Youth Learning

On Their Own Terms

Youth Learning

On Their Own Terms

Creative Practices and Classroom Teaching

Leif Gustavson

Routledge
Taylor & Francis Group
New York   London

Routledge
Taylor & Francis Group
270 Madison Avenue
New York, NY 10016

Routledge
Taylor & Francis Group
2 Park Square
Milton Park, Abingdon
Oxon OX14 4RN

© 2007 by Taylor & Francis Group, LLC
Routledge is an imprint of Taylor & Francis Group, an Informa business

Printed in the United States of America on acid-free paper
10 9 8 7 6 5 4 3 2 1

International Standard Book Number-10: 0-415-95444-4 (Softcover) 0-415-95443-6 (Hardcover)
International Standard Book Number-13: 978-0-415-95444-0 (Softcover) 978-0-415-95443-3 (Hardcover)

Library of Congress Cataloging-in-Publication Data

Gustavson, Leif, 1968-
    Youth learning on their own terms : creative practices and classroom teaching / by Leif Gustavson.
        p. cm. -- (Critical youth studies)
    Includes bibliographical references and index.
    ISBN 978-0-415-95443-3 (hb) -- ISBN 978-0-415-95444-0 (pb)
    1. English language--Study and teaching (Secondary) 2. Youth. 3. Subculture. I. Title.

LB1631.G87 2007
428.0071'273--dc22   2006100538

Visit the Taylor & Francis Web site at
http://www.taylorandfrancis.com

and the Routledge Web site at
http://www.routledge.com

To

Ian, Miguel, and Gil for the amazing work they do and to all teachers who work with their students rather than for or against them

CONTENTS

SERIES EDITOR'S INTRODUCTION

Leif Gustavson's *Youth Learning On Their Own Terms* is a profoundly important and original book. Its impact will surely be felt for years to come. Indeed, Gustavson's book does not so much tell interesting and compelling stories about young people and their everyday creative lives—though it surely does that—as it sets the agenda for a whole, next round of critical scholarship in education. This may seem like a far-reaching claim, but it is entirely warranted. Gustavson carefully traces the out-of-school creative practices of three youth, immersing himself in their complex and multifaceted life-worlds, teasing out how they understand the particulars of their crafts. He asks us to do more than simply acknowledge or "validate" the fact that young people can be creative when left to their own devices. By now, this seems a facile claim. He asks us rather to understand these creative practices in depth and with nuance, including how they intersect with particular classed, raced, and gendered biographies, as they unfold across multiple official and unofficial learning institutions. Working with these particularities allows Gustavson to look at traditional schooling in new and more expansive ways. The complex back-and-forth is at the heart of this text.

In looking beyond formal school sites, Gustavson underscores an impulse as profound as it is basic—most important creative movements and activities ferment in less prescribed ways in nonformal sites. One recalls here the entire history of African American music—from the jook joints that nurtured the blues, to the jazz clubs of the '30s and '40s, to the parks and street corners where hip-hop was born. Each was born out of the needs and concerns of local, disenfranchised communities. Each was born, at least in these cases, in the deep-bodied context of dance and community interaction. One recalls, as well, the range of other creative breakthroughs that mark aesthetic history, including those in literature, visual art, poetry, and beyond. All of these art forms happen because people will them to happen, often in and under oppressive sets of circumstances. While Gustavson's concerns are largely filtered through individual case studies, he raises often marginalized art forms to the forefront of discussion—graffiti writing, zine making and slam poetry, and turntablism. Each of his chapters contains historical and textual analysis that, on its own, would be worthy of scholarly attention.

Yet, Gustavson's highly contextual, case study approach serves him—and us!—quite well. In looking at these creative practices through three very specific biographies, Gustavson highlights their deep and often ignored cognitive components and dimensions. In each of these cases—Ian's zine writing and slam poetry, Miguel's graffiti writing, and Gil's turntable work—we see creative minds at work, making choices and decisions as they work through the intricacies of their media. We see Ian carefully craft his poem, "We are the Sons of John Brown," getting it ready for public performance. We see the bursts of creative decision making, made at unlikely hours of the night. We see him reflect on its successes and failures as he readies another such work for performance. We see Miguel reflect deeply on the history of graffiti writing and its inheritances as he works across multiple kinds of surfaces—public buildings, traditional canvas, and lastly, his own body—dealing with perennial questions about the limits and possibilities inherent in any such form. Finally, we see Gil carefully cull the sonic repository of resources (i.e., record albums), calibrating the ways in which beats work with and against each other, thinking through how song lyrics can be articulated in new and unexpected ways. We see intense moments of transformation here: a gunshot on a *Raiders of the Lost Ark* soundtrack turned into a drumbeat, an obscure song by the Last Poets opened up to critical reflection, sound bites from Malcolm X and Martin Luther King Jr. drawn together in mutually informing ways.

Moreover, Gustavson's deep, ethnographic work highlights the complex and constitutive ways individual classed, raced, and gendered biographies intersect with these projects. We see, for example, the kinds of creative autonomy and freedom that Ian, an affluent white teen, can mobilize when he wants to work on his zine. We see, in stark contrast, how Miguel, a working-class Latino, is constrained by his overcrowded home. He cannot simply follow his creative impulses where and when he wants to—his material circumstances do not allow it. Finally, we see Gil, a working- to middle-class African American teen, struggling to earn money to fund his often expensive craft. We see him, as well, largely on his own. His mother, who heads the household, works long hours in a stressful sales job.

Gustavson thus offers us rich resources here for rethinking, imagining, and reimagining young people's creative lives and pedagogical activities—including where they happen. Indeed, Gil's creative activity takes place in and across a range of sites—his bedroom, the school music room, and the public club among them. The same is true for Ian, who uses his time in school (Model United Nations, in particular) to refine his pieces as he readies to perform at a local venue, the Painted Bride. Miguel, in turn, struggles with and between a range of public and private venues for his work—work that is often explicitly criminalized. For Miguel, school is critical for crystallizing his notion of graffiti as a public art form.

The gesture is key. While some researchers have turned their attention to out-of-school activities, Gustavson's work is in many ways more profound. Instead of "flipping the binary" between in-school and out-of-school learning, he "works the hyphen" between and across the two (Fine, 1994). Gustavson recognizes the continuing value and importance of school sites, as he reads them against nontraditional sites. More than anything, Gustavson's work is intensely *relational*. He does not allow us to rest comfortably on any particular "node" in young people's lives.

All this points to a different model for educators and researchers—one that decenters our authority and control without giving them up entirely and naively. Gustavson shows us a model for thoughtful pedagogy, one that looks toward authentic kinds of assessment and performance, interpretation, and evaluation. These kinds of authentic practices are not the ones often in the foreground and valued in school. They are the kinds that take place in front of real audiences, around the kinds of activities young people value. The charge for educators here is to create or design more nurturing "youthspaces" where such work can flourish. More broadly, though, this work is a generous invitation to look at youth culture and creativity in all their multiplicity, heterogeneity, and specificity. In these and other respects, Gustavson has set the agenda for the next generation of scholars and activists concerned with youth culture today.

Greg Dimitriadis
University at Buffalo, SUNY

REFERENCE

Fine, M. (1994). Working the hyphens: Reinventing self and other in qualitative research. In N. Denzin & Y. Lincoln. (Eds.), *Handbook of qualitative research* (pp. 70–82). Thousand Oaks, CA: Sage Publications.

ACKNOWLEDGMENTS

Writing a book is not a solitary or individual act though it may sometimes look that way from the view of the reader. In truth, writing a book requires the almost miraculous coming together of disparate people who share a desire to help the writer see an idea to clarity and purpose. Throughout the process of writing this book, I was constantly awed and humbled by the generosity and genuine interest of participants, professors, colleagues, friends, editors, and family who were willing to help me wrestle this book to the ground.

First, I would like to express my gratitude to Miguel, Gil, and Ian. This project would not have happened without them. Their willingness to welcome me into their lives was an act of generosity and trust for which I am particularly grateful. This book is a testament to the creative work they do and reflects the relationships we built while completing this research. My thanks to Miguel for his basketball court lessons on graffiti, fashion, and race relations. Thanks to Ian for the late-night French fries and hot chocolate talks about aesthetics and Fugazi; and thanks to Gil for those moments of much-needed focus and direction in terms of the methodology. I am a better teacher, researcher, writer, and person because of them.

I would also like to thank professors Kathleen Hall, Katherine Schultz, Lawrence Sipe, and Shirley Brice Heath. All four helped me conceive of this research idea as a dissertation. Kathy Hall reviewed countless drafts of chapters. I particularly valued the talks we had about ethnography as a way of understanding the lived practices of youth and the conversations we had about the craft of writing research. I wish to thank her for believing in my idea and helping me find a way to make it happen.

I found Kathy Schultz's willingness to share her deep and broad knowledge about literacy and researching with youth incredibly helpful in terms of conceptualizing my study. When we met, I always felt like we were talking writer to writer and teacher to teacher. I also appreciated her patience and guidance in helping me hone my argument. Larry Sipe helped me craft the original proposal and was a necessary stickler for method and analysis. Finally, through her honest critique, Shirley Brice Heath always steered me in a new, more interesting and challenging direction.

Thanks also to my friend and colleague Joe Cytrynbaum. Our weekly fieldwork meetings, numerous phone conferences, and writing partnership moved this idea into book form. I would also like to extend my gratitude to my friend and fellow writer Tyler Doherty for pushing me to allow the youth to speak for themselves in the book. I also want to thank him for our conversations on Richard Rorty, poetics, and the difference between interpretation and appropriation.

Here at Arcadia University, I have had the pleasure of working with Peter Appelbaum. Our collaborations have helped me flesh out and refine how youth culture can inform classroom practice. I am particularly appreciative of our chances to put into practice our shared philosophy through teaching together. Peter's ideas permeate the concluding chapter thanks to our ongoing work around inquiry-based learning and curriculum as infrastructure.

I owe a debt of gratitude to series editor Greg Dimitriadis. I remember presenting a paper that was the seed for this book at a *Journal of Curriculum Theorizing* conference several years ago. There were four people in the audience. Greg was one of them. Over time, Greg invited me to draft a proposal for the book. He was my mentor throughout the process, helping me to craft the proposal and reading several drafts of chapters. I appreciate his vision, intelligence, and support. I would also like to thank Brooke Cosby and Catherine Bernard at Routledge for their editorial skill, guidance, and diligence throughout the publishing process. Whenever I shared my editorial experiences with my colleagues they would inevitably say, "Wow! They're really taking your work seriously. You're lucky!" Yes, I am.

Finally, I would like to thank my family: Kristen, Padgett, and Flannery. Kristen's unwavering belief that I could do it never ceased to amaze me. I am only now beginning to realize how important and calculated her behind-the-scenes support of my work was. Thanks to Padgett for wishing me luck as I walked out the door in the morning to go write, for eagerly making paper airplanes with me out of old drafts of book chapters, and for listening intently at the dinner table as I talked about ideas.

Flannery has grown up with this book. While she may not have known what I was up to in the beginning, her wide smiles and enthusiastic hand clapping, not to mention her proclivity for handing me pens at opportune times, served as necessary pokes and prods to get this book done. Now that she is older, she has perfected the art of asking me, "Are you going to work on your book?" at just the right moment. Thanks also to my parents, Ernest and Julie Gustavson, for asking questions like, "Now, what exactly is it that you are studying?" and "What does that have to do with teaching?" These and other key questions moved me from stammering a thought to making a point.

To everyone, my deepest appreciation.

INTRODUCTION

In the following vignette, we find Ian, the 15-year-old zine writer in this book, burning the midnight oil on his most recent publication. I was up late that night as well, typing fieldnotes and staring out my office window into the dark. It was toward the end of collecting data for this project on how youth work and learn through zine writing, turntablism (the art of using the turntable as a component to make music as well as an instrument to literally play music), and graffiti. Around one in the morning, Ian sent me this e-mail:*

> Leif, I know I said I'd try and arrange it so that you could watch me working on the zine Thursday or something but I've started tonight and I couldn't stop if I wanted to I don't think. I'm sorry about this…but in any event once you start making a zine you have no choice, you gotta make it, it's like all you can do, and I probably won't sleep too much and my math final might suffer but in any event I'm making a zine write now and I've got to work on it.

From the beginning of the project, I had asked Ian if we could schedule a time when I could sit and watch him while he worked on putting together one of his zines (a handmade publication that is printed and distributed by the writer). Every time I made this request, Ian would scrunch up his face and shrug. He would say that he would not mind me watching but scheduling a time would be tough to do because he was never quite sure when he would actually start putting together his

---

* All e-mail, instant message correspondences, and other youth created documents are included in their original spelling and structure for authenticity.

1

zine. "It can happen at any time," he would say. At the end of one of these conversations, we would tentatively agree that he would contact me when he started putting the next one together in the hopes that I could come over and at least catch some of that activity. For this particular zine, all of the work leading up to publishing—the writing of articles, the interviewing, the constructing of collages, and the collecting of peers' writing—pushed Ian to get down on the floor in his bedroom and piece the zine together that night (or, I should say, early morning).

Living an hour away from Ian precluded me from driving over to his house in time to watch him work that night. However, I immediately replied to his message, thanking him for telling me, wishing him luck, and asking if we could talk the next day about the whole process.

The next day, Ian sent me another series of e-mails. This time, they were instant message (IM) chats that he had the night before while he worked on the zine. He introduced them by writing, "They reflect my zine mindset in a lot of ways." One involved a brief exchange with a distant friend of Ian's (whose screen name is Slpunk34), who was having a rough time at home. Ian's screen name is Rebelfunk.

Slpunk34: what's up
Rebelfunk: hey. I'm in the midst of finishing a zine
Slpunk34: sorry for botherin u
Rebelfunk: no, it's cool. I can talk and assemble at the same time. I just
      meant like…like I'm sure you know, assembling a zine is a
      great feeling, it's like being on stage…I think it's better than
      being drunk.

The second IM chat was with a close friend whose screen name is MarxNSparx.

Rebelfunk: i'm in that place, ya know? Like I might not sleep tonight
      and my hands are covered with glue and I'm actually happy
      or at least…i expect you understand this but maybe not
MarxNSparx: kind of, i assume your talking about zine makery?
Rebelfunk: it might be done by the morning…mebe not, I'll try and
      copy it tomorrow afternoon or Friday morning…
MarxNSparx: cool, do you still have notes [for permission to copy the
      zine at school]?
Rebelfunk: I don't have any notes, I'll either sneak in or ask [his history
      teacher] for a note…i don't know if I should work tonight,
      copy tomorrow afternoon, or sleep tonight so I'll be able to
      take math final, work tomorrow afternoon and copy Friday

morning…I don't know if i can sleep when i'm trying to work…then I'm isolated

MarxNSparx: yeah, screw that whole zinester thing, it's not going any-where, you should find a career in math

Rebelfunk: yes, math is real, emotions are arbitrary

MarxNSparx: im hoping to get shot this summer [referring to a youth program in Israel]

Rebelfunk: orwell makes it sound like fun [in *Homage to Catalonia*]… but I still think it's a bad idea.

Ian's e-mail to me and the two IM chats quoted above provide an entry point for the focus of this book. This book is about the complex work and learning that 15-year-old youth do on their own terms through what I call *creative practices*. I see creative practice as a hybrid of Aristotle's notion of *tekhne* and Paul Willis's theory of common culture. Aristotle defines *tekhne* as "the art in mundane skill and, more significantly, in day-to-day life…an intrinsic aesthetic or crafting that underlies the practices of everyday life…'a reasoned habit of mind in making something'" (Cintron, 1997, p. xii). According to Willis (1998), common culture is the everyday practice of producing popular culture products like graffiti murals, zines, and turntable pieces. Ian's practice of zine writing, for example, is a part of his everyday life. He literally carries it with him wherever he goes. Articles and pieces for future zines line the sides of notes that he takes in English class. Ian spends hours and days asking friends to submit work, editing his own writing, and laying out pages. His zine writing takes him to film festivals, concerts, and bookstores among other places where he knows he will find people and texts that are interesting and will inform his work. These actions of Ian's, to me, are the "intrinsic aesthetic or crafting that underlies the practice of everyday life." And through this conscious and unconscious "mapping" and constructing of his everyday life, Ian produces common culture. Ian's creative practice is part of who he is and how he understands the world around him. The way he lives his life informs his zine making and his zine making influences the way in which he lives day to day.

This book teases out the habits of mind and body—the "intrinsic aesthetic *and* crafting"—that enable youth like Ian to do this kind of work. It documents and analyzes the skills and concepts that make it possible for youth to work and learn through creative practices. From the IM conversations above, one can see how Ian's practice involves a multiplicity of sources and spaces. There is the George Orwell reference that Ian makes at the end of the second chat, which connects his friends' life to a canonical writer of the 20th century. There is the strategic planning for how Ian is going to get the zine photocopied: He can either get a note from his history teacher or sneak in to use the copier on Friday. There is the aesthetic talk about art and what it means to be an artist: Ian makes the cynical comment about the privilege of rationality (math) over emotions (art); he is excited by the glue all over his hands; and he revels in the intensity of the work and the idea that he might not sleep that night because of the momentum he feels to create something. There is the tension between the need Ian feels for publishing his zine and the demands of schoolwork (e.g., his math final). When reading these IM chats, I get the sense that the conversations themselves are necessary creative stimuli for the production of Ian's zines.

This book is also about the tension between idiosyncratic ways of working and the often prescribed and decontextualized ways of working and learning found in many schools. In my 16 years of teaching middle and secondary school students as well as teaching teachers of elementary, middle, and secondary students, I have become acutely aware of the disconnect between the ways in which many school districts and schools design learning environments and the ways in which youth design learning environments for themselves; one example is the way writing is traditionally taught.

Writing is often taught in terms of a skill by means of a linear process. The writing process is presented as brainstorming, prewriting, creating a first draft, sharing, editing, completing a final draft, and publishing. Writing assignments are presented linearly as well. Students are to work on one piece of writing at a time and finish that piece of writing before moving on to the next piece. Often there is little to no connection between the two other than the fact that both pieces of writing involve commenting on something that they have read. Not surprisingly, Ian employs this writing strategy as you will see in a later chapter. However, he does not use it in a linear fashion: brainstorming to prewriting to drafting, etc. Instead, his writing process is discontinuous, meaning that one phase of the writing process does not necessarily follow another; revising and brainstorming take place simultaneously, for example. Performance does not only happen at the end of the process. He is constantly performing midproduction in order to get feedback. The reified writing process practiced in many schools seems artificial and manufactured in light of the ways in which the youth in this book work. We need to think of our pedagogy as being a vehicle through which youth like Gil, Ian, and Miguel—the three young men I focus on in this book—can bring their "intrinsic" skills to bear on classroom learning. More important, we must have these "reasoned habits of mind" influence how we design the learning environment in the first place.

This can happen by shifting our sense of a learning environment as an imposed structure to an infrastructure. Pedagogy as a structure is static and not generative. Students must fit in to constraints constructed by the teacher, school, or district. Therefore, the possibilities for ways of working and what can be learned are constrained within the parameters of the class. Often, when teaching and learning are considered a structure, the outcome of the learning is predetermined, like a biology or chemistry lab where the result is known before the students do the experiment, or a worksheet students must fill out that will *prepare* them to write a story. More broadly, school district core curricula are often enacted as structures. There is a specific set of skills and conceptual knowledge that must be acquired within a prescribed amount of time and the methods for developing these skills and conceptual knowledge are determined by people other than the teachers (school administration, district superintendents, and textbook companies).

Conversely, pedagogy as infrastructure is dynamic and generative. Students build off the framework of the class, utilizing tacit skills and conceptual knowledge to build new skills and knowledge. Pedagogy as infrastructure is designed around rituals, habits of mind and body, and criteria. The objective of the learning is not for everyone to arrive at the same conclusion. Instead, students are pushed to take individual action on what they have learned (Perkins, 1993; Starnes & Paris, 2000; Wiggins, 1989). Perkins writes, "education must aim for active use of knowledge and skill....Students garner knowledge and skill in schools so that they can put them to work in professional roles—scientist, engineer, designer, doctor, businessperson, writer, artist, musician—and in lay roles—citizen, voter, parent—that require appreciation, understanding, and judgment" (p. 28). Pedagogy as infrastructure views the work of the class extending beyond the four walls of the classroom and into the "real world." It focuses on developing scaffolds for how work will get done in the classroom. This book works to show what a classroom infrastructure looks like that sees the way youth work on their own terms as a shared form of practice that enables the class to meet the pressures of institutional and district curricular mandates.

You will notice throughout this book that I use the term *design* when discussing pedagogy and curriculum. I believe, like Wiggins and McTighe (2005), that teachers are designers of learning experiences. What happens in the classroom should not be magic or happenstance. Instead, it should be the result of intentional planning by the teachers and the students. Wiggins and McTighe define *design* thusly:

To plan the form and structure of something or the pattern or motif of a work of art. In education, teachers are designers in both senses, aiming to develop purposeful, coherent, effective, and engaging lessons, units, and courses of study and accompanying assessments to achieve identified results. To say that something happens by design is to say that it occurs through thoughtful planning as opposed to by accident or by "winging it." (2005, p. 340)

This book, in part, is designed to help teachers thoughtfully plan lessons, units, and courses of study informed by a working knowledge of how youth work and learn on their own terms. We must acknowledge the skills and complex problem-solving strategies of these practices in order to be able to translate that understanding into informing our teaching and into designing learning environments for and with our students. Youth have much to teach us about how to teach. Shultz and Cook-Sather argue that if we truly want to take school reform seriously, we must "understand...what and how education means, looks, and feels to [youth]" (2001, p. 2). In their case, they refer to the ways in which youth understand and participate in school learning. However, I think we can extend Shultz and Cook-Sather's sentiment to the everyday lives of youth as well. We need to understand what learning means, looks like, and feels like in their everyday lives if we are to create meaningful schools and be excellent teachers. This book seeks to find ways to (re)introduce youth's habits of mind and body into how learning is done in school settings.

In order to merge these two ideas—an in-depth understanding of the creative practices of youth and informing pedagogy through the ways youth work—I offer ethnographic case studies of three 15-year-old males from different ethnic (Ian is Caucasian, Miguel is Puerto Rican–American, and Gil is African American) and class backgrounds. Each of the three youth engages in a particular kind of work: Miguel is a graffiti writer who also explores fly tying, model building, and tattooing; Gil is a turntablist; and Ian is a zine writer. I show how and why these youth work the way they do and then focus on certain aspects of that work that I feel can influence how we design learning environments as teachers. When youth work "on their own terms"—meaning that they engage in some form of ongoing practice without adult supervision or guidance—they tend to work reflectively and experimentally. They also engage in multiple forms of performance as a means to evaluate and strategize their work. Youth who work on their own terms have multiple projects going on simultaneously, one taking precedence over another at different times in the production process. Often these simultaneous projects feed off of one another. Youth engaged in these forms of work have a sense of the history of their practice. They are able to tell the story of the history of their craft and point to key figures within that history that have informed their practice. This history informs their aesthetic style and the content of their work. Youth are also able to articulate how the history of their craft influences the way they practice. Finally, youth like Ian, Miguel, and Gil also constantly interpret through their creative practices. The act of interpretation enables youth to evaluate their own work as well as construct meaning out of other people's work. It is these skills of youth practice that should in part *become* the practice of working and learning in classrooms.

If we are to create, support, and sustain schools that are meaningful and rigorous learning spaces for youth, we—teachers, administrators, and parents—need to cultivate genuine interests in the ways youth work and learn in their everyday lives. Zine writing, graffiti, and turntablism—all types of work that youth pursue on their own terms and often outside officially sanctioned adult spaces of learning—offer rich insights into the ways youth work and learn when they ask questions that they want to pursue, develop projects that they want to complete, and perform products of this work to communities of peers and mentors. To be relevant, responsive, and critically engaged, a 21st-century pedagogy must develop a deep knowledge of these youth processes of work and learn to embody them in classroom teaching and curriculum. How can the work of youth influence educators in designing learning environments that are rigorous, interesting, and personally meaningful for both youth *and* teachers? This book works to address this question from the perspective of a teacher and parent fascinated by the creative lives of youth.

WHY TURNTABLISM, ZINE WRITING, AND GRAFFITI?

I chose turntablism, zine writing, and graffiti as creative practices to study because they are often part of the everyday lives of youth and they are rarely ever considered valuable parts of a school curriculum. We could add other youth practices to this list as well: skateboarding, breakdancing, clubbing, video-game playing, and tricking out cars, for example. It is not the kind of creative practice that is important; it is the complex process of work behind the practice that I contend can inform and influence the way we work and learn with students in schools. In other words, I am not advocating co-opting these practices as subject matter or units of study. Instead, we need to learn from the ways in which youth work within art forms like zine writing, turntablism, and graffiti, and then allow these ways of working to influence how we talk, write, compute, read, plan, and literally *be* with students in our classrooms. We need to construct learning environments where the unique learning styles inherent in these practices are honored and understood.

More often than not, the processes by which students engage in turntablism, zine writing, and graffiti (along with other creative practices) exist outside of school-sanctioned ways of learning. Therefore, in order for them to exist, youth must dedicate a considerable amount of their everyday lives to keep this work going, sometimes even at the expense of their schoolwork. They also find ways to import creative work into the place many youth spend most of their waking hours: school. In addition, these creative practices demonstrate a desire on the part of youth to determine their own learning trajectories. Youth navigate large cities without drivers' licenses, maintain networks of fellow artisans, strategize how to obtain equipment, and find ways to create with few resources. They want to, need to, and must work and learn on their own terms. Some youth do this through a refusal to attend school altogether; others make school a part of their wider learning worlds. They recognize the interdependence of the role school plays with other learning spaces. Schools no longer, and perhaps never did, occupy a monolithic position, separate from the rest of youth's learning lives.

Most young people are engaged in some kind of creative practice that is not an adult-supervised afterschool activity. Whether it is blogging, video gaming, shopping, TV watching, clubbing, collecting and burning music, or redesigning spaces like their rooms, most youth are involved in some kind of practice of their own making that involves a community of practice (actual and imagined), rituals, materials, skills, and tacit knowledge. They involve performance, experimentation, evaluation, reflection, and interpretation. It behooves us as educators and parents to tune in to these practices and think critically about what they can teach us about teaching and learning.

My personal interest in conducting this study came from working with students in classrooms and witnessing the creative work they were doing outside school. Before returning to pursue a Ph.D. in education, I taught middle school English/language arts for seven years. During that time I established numerous work relationships with students who engaged in what I thought were extremely interesting activities. As my students clued me in to what they were up to outside of school, I started organizing my seventh-grade class in such a way that many of these students could bring their outside projects into class to develop and share with others. These projects ranged from writing computer code for online adventure games, composing music for various musical instruments, or sculpting to drafting scripts for one-act plays, painting, or building stereo speakers. Years later, some of these students—including two youth in this book—continued to stay in touch with me. They kept me abreast of their current activity, often sending me work they thought I would be interested in. At first I considered what these teens did as "hobbies" or "passing fancies," but in conversation with these teens, I learned that it was much more than that. These teens were incredibly passionate about what they did, eager to talk about it, and complex in their conversations about it.

While diligently and sometimes not so diligently going about their schoolwork for my class, youth were producing fantastic work out of school. They constructed sophisticated processes in order to do the work, fashioning a language in which to communicate with others, continuously representing themselves in refreshing ways as readers, writers, mathematicians, scientists, and historians. These practices also challenged my assumptions about what a class should look and feel like. They helped me realize that the ways in which I designed how we learned in the class often excluded students who worked really hard outside of my classroom. They made me question my role as the teacher. By allowing my students to bring their work into the classroom and talking about that work with them, they showed me what a productive learning environment could look like if it was more finely tuned to the ways youth design meaningful work for themselves.

Over time my practice shifted. I pulled myself away from the center of the experience and worked to create an atmosphere of collaboration in the classroom. I worked to consider my students and me *as* mathematicians, scientists, historians, and writers instead of as *students of* these disciplines. I built into the class ways of getting to know how we all worked, learned, and created. I reflected more on how I worked on my own terms. I then used what I learned from these conversations and reflections to design units, daily activities, and forms of assessment that capitalized on the idiosyncratic ways in which we worked. I also moved away from designing work where I was the sole audience as teacher. Instead, part of my criteria for the work of the class would be for students to "put what they learned back out into the world." In other words, students needed to take action on what they learned with an audience other than me or the class. This "real-world" audience provided opportunities for more authentic forms of critique for the work. Finally, I realized that I needed to work alongside my students. It was no longer acceptable for me to sit back and watch my students work for me. I needed to be a mathematician, scientist, historian, or writer with them, and be engaged in the same issues, problems, and projects in which my students were involved.

This shift in my pedagogy fundamentally changed the work dynamic in my classroom. Students who were usually disenchanted with the class were now excited to be there. The overall quality of the work improved. Students became better critics of each other's, and my, work. They worked harder and made commitments with outside audiences, which they kept. What was perhaps most satisfying about this kind of work was the way students discussed it in their self-assessment letters at the end of the semester. They wrote things like, "I learned how to trust myself"; "I plan to take everything I learned this year into other classes"; "Perhaps the first major lesson that I learned…is that true work comes from the inside…if you make the effort, take the time, think, analyze, write, do it all over again, and then take time to eat and sleep, the work will come."

This book is my attempt to contribute to the broad and long conversation around teaching and learning by merging youth's "reasoned habit[s] of mind and making something" into the daily, weekly, monthly, and yearly design of the classroom.

Ian, Gil, and Miguel

The nature of this work—looking at practices of cultural production over time—demands a small unit of study. The best way I could research this form of youth work in depth, across domains, and over time was to narrow my focus to three youth. Over the course of the year and several months that I spent with them, I circumnavigated the city, following wherever the youth work took us: schools, clubs, stores, friends' basements, studios, fishing lakes, churches, open mic readings, basketball courts, restaurants, and their bedrooms. I also chose to work with three youth from different cultural backgrounds as a way of exploring how this kind of work is created across race, class, geographical, and school experiences. I chose not to work with young women in this study because of the potential logistical challenges inherent in cross-gender ethnographic work. I spent many hours driving the "boys" around alone in the car. I also spent a lot of time in the participants' bedrooms watching them work. This kind of shadowing would have been considerably more difficult had I attempted to shadow young women. My focus on the creative practices of young men should in no way be read as an indication that only young men do this kind of work. Quite the contrary, young women do this kind of work and there is some interesting recent writing on it (Ganz & McDonald, 2006; Skelton, 2001; Skelton & Valentine, 1998; Taormino & Green, 1997).

I taught Ian and Gil when they were in seventh grade. Ian had started his zine, *The Antisocial*, and was shooting films on a fairly regular basis, and Gil was developing an intense interest in music, particularly guitar. Both included me in this work, showing me what they were doing. Ian, 15 years old and Caucasian, lived in a middle-class suburb of Philadelphia with his mother, father, and sister. His house was tucked away in a maze of streets that led out to a main thoroughfare. Ian's mother is Lutheran and his father is Jewish. Ian expressed an interest in both religions. He attended Hebrew school as well as confirmation classes. Ian went to an elite, private school that was a considerable commute from his house. His mother drove him to school because he did not have his driver's license at the time of the research. The location of the school also meant that most of his friends did not live near him. Therefore, he spent a lot of his free time around where his friends lived or in Philadelphia.

While I got the sense that many of Ian's teachers considered Ian to be bright, Ian was not doing particularly well in school. In his own words, he described his work as being "all right," mostly B's. This did not concern him. He told me that he was more concerned with learning than with a grade. While Ian cobbled together work in the summer as well as volunteering at a soup kitchen in the city, he did not work or volunteer during the school year. School took up most of his time. This frustrated Ian because he would have liked to continue volunteering during the year. He also mentioned that school curtailed his production of zines because when he got home he needed to do his homework rather than publish his own work.

A watershed moment for me as a teacher was when Ian, as a seventh grader, brought in a comic book that he was designing. He sat down in the middle of the floor of our classroom and started working on it, cutting out little pieces of construction paper and gluing them together to make the comic book characters. Other students huddled around him and asked what he was doing, commenting on the process and getting involved in the construction. This event was the beginning of my education on how to introduce the work that my students were doing outside of school into the curriculum of our class.

Gil, 15 years old and African American, lived with his mother just within the western border of Philadelphia, a stone's throw away from the elite, private school that he and Ian attended. Gil's mother sold medical insurance to senior citizens—an incredibly demanding and stressful job because of the weekly quota that she had to make. Gil worked hard during the summer before the research in order to help pay for an exchange trip to Spain offered through the school that coming year as well as for equipment he wanted to buy for his turntablism. He also worked during the school year, picking up a few hours bagging groceries at a nearby grocery store, as well as DJing for some parties. In terms of academics, Gil was doing very well. He registered for an advanced class in math to his mother's surprise and pleasure. At the beginning of the research, Gil took his studies seriously and appreciated the positive feedback he received from teachers and peers regarding his schoolwork.

As a graduate student, I worked with Ian on a research project involving students' perceptions of computers and technologies and found him to be an incredibly insightful and dependable participant in the research. I worked with Gil on a research project as well, investigating student identity formation in school. He proved equally reliable, working with me on multiple drafts of the essay. What I found most invigorating about this work with them were their ability to challenge me on observations that I made about them and their willingness to question the research and its purpose. Not so coincidentally, these two studies provided further insight into the creative practices of teenagers and exposed ethical difficulties inherent in collaborative research with youth (Gustavson & Cytrynbaum, 2003). Perhaps the most challenging aspect of researching with teens is designing a study that indeed supports and utilizes group wisdom, not only in the collecting of data but in the writing of the book as well. After both projects, Ian and Gil spoke with me, critiquing the products and processes of the work and outlining what they felt could be done to improve both in the future. This present study implements many of Gil and Ian's previous suggestions.

Miguel, 15 years old and Puerto Rican, lived in North Philadelphia with his mother and her boyfriend of many years. Miguel's biological father lived not too far from him, and he saw him often. There were many other relatives and friends who stayed with Miguel and his mother on a regular basis, at which time Miguel either shared or gave his bedroom to whomever was visiting, much to Miguel's chagrin. Miguel's mom worked in the bakery of a wholesale superstore 40 minutes from where they lived. Her boyfriend, whom Miguel considered to be his "real" father, was a maintenance man for a motel near the airport. At the inception of this research, the court had just erased Miguel's graffiti charge. He was finishing up his probation at a local youth center and was having a tough time at school. He did not feel challenged by the material, having been moved to a lower-track class. He told me that he had tried to get himself moved up but that the teacher and the principal had told him that there was no more room in the advanced class. The class he was in had 36 students. Miguel often missed classes because of the need he felt to accompany his mother and sister to the doctor. These visits happened often because both his mother and sister were frequently ill. Miguel did not feel well himself, often complaining of feeling tired. I came to see this as exhaustion stemming from the auto mechanic and construction work he did with his brothers in order to help his family make ends meet.

I had never worked with Miguel before this study. I heard of him from a colleague who suggested that the way in which Miguel talked about his graffiti sounded similar to how Ian and Gil spoke of their work. From that recommendation, I called Miguel and we met. He showed me his work and told me of his interest in old school graffiti, giving me a brief but in-depth lesson on the differences in style between old and new school. I could tell from his passionate interest in talking about his graffiti and his overall historical knowledge of the art form that the discourse he was in the process of developing would fit nicely with the others. Most important, Miguel, like Ian and Gil, wanted to talk about his work. Graffiti is one of the more maligned youth creative practices in part because it is illegal. I felt that including a practitioner of the craft in this study could possibly shed new light on the art form and its relation to learning and school.

This book takes the somewhat unusual stance of seeing hope in the current system of public schooling. With the rise of critical pedagogy, we have become well versed in the language of oppression and social injustice in relation to public schools. By now, the concepts of hidden curricula, hegemony, the banking system of education, and cultural reproduction are almost clichés. While this important work has drawn attention to serious oversights in our understanding of how students learn or are prevented from learning, I think it is important not to lose sight of the sites of possibility within the current system. I am not advocating the draconian approach of No Child Left Behind, with its total disregard of child development and its fear tactic approach to school reform, but rather I acknowledge that there are teachers in classrooms with students right now that are doing personally meaningful and rigorous work. They are living and acting within this system every day. One more book that shows how awful their situation is is not useful. In this regard, we need to avoid the stance of what Richard Rorty in his book *Achieving Our Country* (1999) calls the "spectatorial, disgusted, mocking left," which essentially has lost hope with current systems and institutions, and instead adopt Rorty's idea of the progressive left: a left that focuses on "specific social practices and specific changes in those practices" (p. 35). The former stance is a disenchanted thumbing of the nose at the current system. The latter positions researchers, teachers, administrators, parents, and students as agents of curricular and pedagogical change rather than as mere spectators of an imposed process. We *are* capable of making change, and we have a catalyst for this change. In the case of this book, what we have to build on is the creative impulses of youth.

If we are to truly support our youth as lifelong learners, we must take into account and have a deep understanding of the practices that they develop themselves in order to grow as learners. We need to do this because youth are using any and every means to create meaning regardless of whether or not we acknowledge that they are doing so. They are pulling from their out-of-school reading of media and weaving it into their reading of school texts in order to construct meaning. They are using out-of-school writing habits, sometimes in opposition to school-sanctioned writing behaviors for writing. If we were to acknowledge that the ways in which youth conceptualize themselves as readers and writers specifically, and as learners more broadly, are built out of creative work both in and outside of school, then I believe we have a better chance of working with youth to conceptualize themselves as lifelong learners.

These creative practices I document are important for educational researchers and educators to consider for several reasons. Often these creative practices take precedence over schoolwork and therefore are rich sites for understanding the ways in which youth learn "on their own terms." Gil, for example, would come home from school and practice on his turntables for six hours, taking a quick break to grab some dinner. The ways in which these youth appropriate time and space in school to do these creative practices disrupts the distinction often made in educational research of learning that occurs inside and outside of school. Much schooling today frames the idea of learning as an objective activity that is primarily done within school. School then becomes the only space considered necessary to acquire knowledge. Youth must *go* to school in order to *get* knowledge. However, I argue that youth construct knowledge through interacting with a multitude of spaces, people, and media. Research consistently shows how the "unsanctioned" literacy practices of youth (like graffiti and zine writing) are already a part of the subaltern literacy of the classroom (Camitta, 1993; Moje, 2002). Therefore, it seems appropriate that the next step in thinking about how to blend these practices with pedagogy is to find ways of lifting youth's creative practices out of their subaltern status and into the light of the classroom. In short, I argue that teachers need to consider the ways in which youth build communities of practice as well as how youth are reflective, experimental, performative, evaluative, and interpretive when considering how the practice of teaching can be informed by what constitutes a rigorous and meaningful learning environment.

Throughout this introduction, I have made reference to a set of skills that I see youth developing and employing in their creative practices across race and class lines. I would like to spend a moment here defining these terms so that readers have a clear understanding of how I use them in relation to the creative practices discussed in this book.

YOUTH HABITS OF MIND AND BODY IN CREATIVE PRACTICES

Communities of Practice

First and foremost, in order to sustain their creative practices, youth are involved in making connections with groups of people who share their interests. These groups are commonly called "communities of practice." According to Jean Lave and Etienne Wenger, a community of practice is "a set of relations among persons, activity, and world, over time and in relation with other tangential and overlapping communities of practice. A community of practice is an intrinsic condition for the existence of knowledge, not least because it provides the interpretive support necessary for making sense of its heritage" (Lave & Wenger, 1991, p. 98). A community of practice is a group of people connected through a shared interest in an activity.

This community of practice is not isolated in its work, according to Lave and Wenger. Instead, it is connected and overlaps with other communities of practice. For example, a skateboarder would not only be connected to a community of skateboarders, he or she would also more than likely be connected to other communities of practice such as snowboarders, musicians, BMX bikers, groups interested in particular music, etc. These different and linked communities of practice contribute in varying ways to the development and evolution of specific creative practices.

A community of practice, according to Lave and Wenger, is the engine of knowledge production within a creative practice. Part of that knowledge is a shared understanding of the work: where it comes from, how it started, who are the important ancestors of the craft, what is the specific language of the craft, etc. Communities of practice come together physically, like when Ian, the zine writer, gets together with other poets to put on a poetry slam. They also "meet" virtually through IM chats, mobile phone text messaging, and Web sites such as MySpace. Another form of virtual meeting is through the way in which youth imagine collaboration with luminaries within their chosen creative practice. For example, Miguel, the graffiti writer, identifies himself with well-known graffiti artists in Philadelphia and beyond. This identification influences the style choices he makes within his own graffiti practice. It is safe to say that individuals would not be able to sustain their chosen creative practice without the physical and virtual communities of practitioners that share their passions and interests.

Experimentation

Experimentation is the sometimes spontaneous, sometimes calculated enactment of ideas in one's craft. In relation to the creative practices of youth, I see a connection between experimentation and improvisation. In a conversation on the difference between composition and improvisation, composer Karlheinz Essl defines improvisation in this way:

> The significant difference between composition and improvisation is their different dealing with time. In composition you are in a way outside time, abstracting therefrom [*sic*]; one tries to imagine the whole process and can zero in on time microscopically—stop it, so to speak. In composition you simulate a time structure that—converted into reality—lets the actual piece come into being. But improvisation is completely different: you are inside time in the moment, form time and its passing in "real time"; and now, within this mercilessly passing time frame you have to follow a certain way which maybe you've thought about before or which turns out to be negotiable during the improvisation, and at the same time be continuously conscious of references: what's happened before, how can I go on working with this. This is no senseless continuous going forward, but the intentional visiting of previously existing conditions in order to further transform them. Again and again building bridges to the past. I think this is very important: that time goes forward, but in improvisation again and again one tries consciously to recur to that which was, so as to create points of reference. (2006, para. 2)

Improvisation, like some experimentation, is of the moment. One is forced to follow a path that one has decided on the split second before. Essl says that in improvising, one needs to keep in mind where one has been before within the piece as well as in a constant state of evaluation, determining whether the chosen path is the right one. Improvisation also involves returning to previous moves or decisions to revisit them in a way and change them, morph them into something new. To Essl, improvisation is iterative. It builds on previous moves or decisions. It reinterprets what has happened before. These returns are crucial for they establish what Essl calls "points of reference"—signposts that the musician, in this case, can return to for guidance. The creative works of the youth within this book involve both spontaneous and calculated experimentation, whether it be Gil's split-second decision to try a particular scratch on his turntables or Miguel's measured decision to try his graffiti on canvas as opposed to on a cinder-block wall. A crucial element in this youth work is the willingness to experiment to see where it might take their work.

Experimenting is the willingness to try things in one's craft without knowing whether or not they will work. One experiments based on previous work within the craft. Prior knowledge enables one to try new things. Another way of thinking about experimentation is as trial and error. Reinsmith (1997) writes of the link between trial and error and learning:

> No trial and error, no experimentation, then no real learning. The learner needs to fool with things, to try them on, to adjust and readjust. This is true whether dealing with concrete skills or with conceptualizing. The "fit" will come eventually since our minds are by nature meaning-oriented. (p. 7)

According to Reinsmith (1997), people instinctively want to make meaning out of experience. In order for meaning to occur, people need freedom to fiddle around with new ideas and new objects, to try ideas that they have, and to—perhaps most important—make mistakes. These mistakes are what enable people to refine ideas and attempt something else. It is in this refining and course altering that one develops understandings regarding skills or concepts.

Evaluation and Assessment

I find Wiggins and McTighe's definition of both evaluation and assessment to be applicable when considering the creative practices of these youth. They write, "by assessment we mean the act of determining the extent to which the desired results are on the way to being achieved and to what extent they have been achieved" (Wiggins & McTighe, 2005, p. 6). Assessment, to Wiggins and McTighe, is ongoing feedback. Assessment provides the worker with a picture of how she or he is doing and what needs to be done in order to accomplish the desired outcome. They make it a point to separate assessment and evaluation. In fact, they caution against making the two terms synonymous. While assessment is ongoing feedback on performance, evaluation, to Wiggins and

McTighe, is "more summative." They connect evaluation with a grade or a result. Evaluation places a value on the outcome. I see the youth engaging in both of these skills through their work.

In terms of the creative practices described in this book, evaluation means a value placement of one's work, a subconscious or conscious judging of one's work based on a set of criteria. These criteria are based on a shared understanding of a level of quality of work constructed by communities of practice. Evaluation occurs during practice and after performance. It is both formative and summative in youth creative practices. Evaluation can be internal or personal, meaning that youth can evaluate the work themselves. Or it can be provided by an outside individual or audience. Evaluation is a critical take on one's work—the physicality of it as well as the meaning behind it—with a two-fold objective: (1) to push the work forward in challenging or meaningful ways and (2) to judge the work on its effectiveness.

Interpretation

Ricoeur writes, "Interpretation…is the work of thought which consists in deciphering the hidden meaning in the apparent meaning, in unfolding the levels of meaning implied in the literal meaning" (1974, p. 13). According to Ricoeur, there are multiple layers of meaning within any "text." Interpretation is constructing an understanding of the multiple meanings underneath that obvious or surface meaning. Texts can be poems, turntable compositions, or graffiti pieces. They can be films, clothing, or facial expressions. One can interpret the meaning behind why a particular word is used or phrase of music is sampled. One can interpret the audience response to a piece or product that he or she performs. One can also interpret the effectiveness of another person's craft—the way he or she goes about doing the particular creative practice. Evaluation and assessment are forms of interpretation. Finally, and perhaps most interesting in terms of this study, interpretation is how youth interpret the work of others *through* their art form. In other words, they communicate the meaning of another text, object, or image through their chosen form of expression.

Performance

The habits described above are interrelated. Youth employ them in conjunction with one another in order to make their creative practices happen. As I will show, youth's communities of practice provide "venues" for evaluation and assessment to take place. Interpretation opens up avenues for experimentation. Another habit that cannot be undervalued is performance. Kapferer, in Dufrenne, defines performance as "a unity of text and enactment, neither being reducible to the other. More properly, it is what certain philosophers of aesthetic experience refer to as the Work, irreducible to its performance and yet graspable only through them or, rather, in them" (Dufrenne, 1973, p. 27).

Here, performance means the blending of a text and the acting out of that text. According to Kapferer, one cannot separate the two. The text depends on the enactment and the enactment depends on the text. In other words, the text is only understandable through the performing of it and vice versa. I am intrigued by the use of the term *work* here. I understand Kapferer's use of the term to mean that one can only understand the process of creation through witnessing a performance or product that is a result of that process. This definition of performance has interesting implications for teaching and learning. Perhaps through designing opportunities for students to truly perform, teachers will develop a better understanding of the work and learning involved in getting to that performance (see Wiggins & McTighe, 2005).

While one is performing a product within a creative practice, the person is also performing what it means to be a spoken word artist, turntablist, or graffiti writer, for example. This aspect of performing is an important part of developing into a "legitimate" turntablist, zine writer, or graffiti artist. One is not only performing what it means to be a turntablist, for example, when he or she is sharing a product with an audience. Goffman suggests that performance is "all the activity of an individual which occurs during a period marked by his continuous presence before a particular set of observers and which has some influence on the observers" (1990, p. 22). Therefore, the clothes one wears, the words one chooses to use, and the way one walks are performance acts as well. They, in part, serve to define what it means to look like, sound like, and be like a turntablist.

Reflection

What I hope to convey here is the level of consciousness within the work youth choose to do. Youth are not blindly or ignorantly going about being graffiti artists, zine writers, or turntablists. Miguel, Ian, and Gil are mindful of the work that they are doing. An aspect of their work that fuels them is the act of interpreting their own practice. This form of interpretation aids them in developing a knowledge of the work and a theory for why they do what they do.

Part of this mindfulness comes from a consistent practice of reflecting on their creative work. Self-reflection is a form of interpretation through introspection. It is the process of making personal meaning out of actions, work, and things done within one's practice. It is the ability to look back at something one has done and personally critique it in an effort to both evaluate its effectiveness as well as to plan what should happen next. Oftentimes, reflection happens within the mind. It is a process of thinking about what one has done. However, reflection can happen in IM chats and e-mails as well. What others say and do can trigger one to think introspectively about his or her own actions. The youth in this book reflect regularly on the way they develop the skills of their craft as well as on how others react to their performances.

As I mentioned above, these habits of mind and body are interrelated and integrated. I will show how performance makes it possible for youth to interpret and reflect and how communities of practice provide outlets for performance and experimentation. At times a certain habit may take the foreground in order for the youth to accomplish a specific task or goal, but other habits are at play in these times as well. In fact, it is the interrelation and integration of these habits of mind and body that enable the youth to do the work that they do.

I would also like to add that these habits occur within the creative practices of youth regardless of socioeconomic status. In the beginning of my research, I assumed that these habits would be more prevalent or more refined in the creative practices of middle- and upper-middle-class youth because of their access to particular ways of knowing and material resources. This turned out not to be the case. Youth from different class backgrounds do employ the habits in different ways and for different reasons, as I will show, but there was striking similarity in how the youth fundamentally went about doing their work. This is an exciting finding for me, because it lends more weight to the argument that learning environments that are designed around deficit models of teaching, or that view youth from particular backgrounds as lacking essential skills or knowledge, do ignore the talents and competencies that most students bring to the classroom.

THE CHAPTERS

The first three chapters focus on how Ian, Gil, and Miguel engage in their respective creative practices. Specifically, I show the ways in which performance, experimentation, communities of practice, evaluation and assessment, reflection, and interpretation make their creative practices happen. Each of these chapters opens with a brief history of the creative practice as a way of defining it, of supplying a historical context for the work in which the three youth are engaged, and to illustrate how these art forms are distinctly youth driven. In the course of spending over a year with Gil, Miguel, and Ian, it became clear that the histories of these creative practices were important parts of the foundation of their work. Within these histories are communities of practitioners who laid the philosophical and technical groundwork for their contemporary practices. Miguel, Gil, and Ian drew from these histories in everything from casual conversation in which they invoked particular practitioners of the art form; references they made in the products of their craft; artifacts they collected that related to their work; to the conscious creative conventions that they either adopted or reacted against.

For Ian, we can go back to the 1940s when poets hand-published small books of their poetry. I trace turntablism back to the beginnings of hip-hop in the mid-1960s. For the purposes of this study, I link Miguel's graffiti practice to the piecing of trains in the late 1970s to the mid-1980s in New York City because it is the history with which Miguel most identifies. Ian, Gil, and Miguel use their knowledge of these histories to shape their own communities of practice, inform the content of their crafts, and develop processes for doing their work.

In Chapter 1, "Multiple Writing (Con)texts: The Writing Life of a Zine Maker," I chronicle Ian's creative practice as a zine writer and spoken word artist over the course of a year and a half. I show how Ian became interested in zine writing and spoken word through a developing interest in the history of the art form and interest in writers who were publishing at the time. I then show how performance plays an integral role in how Ian develops as a zine writer and spoken word artist. I do this by focusing on the evolution of one of Ian's poems: "We are the Sons of John Brown." Finally, I show how his public performance of "We are the Sons of John Brown" pushes him into other spaces and experiences that broaden his creative practice as well as his community of practice. Throughout this chapter, I analyze how Ian's reflective habit and various performances enable him to continually evaluate the products within his practice.

Chapter 2, "The Shifting Creative Practices of a Puerto Rican–American Youth," looks at the trajectory of Miguel's creative practice by discussing the development of his craft as a graffiti writer, arguing that the interplay of a community of practice—in the form of friends, family, and graffiti heroes—and Miguel's sense of the history of the art form mediate the development of this way of being a graffiti writer. Next, I show how Miguel's skills of reflection and evaluation enable him to critically read his current situation as a graffiti writer, which prompts him to move to represent his graffiti on canvas and eventually to giving up graffiti altogether. Finally, the chapter ends with Miguel's shift to tattooing his skin. A vignette of Miguel's brother giving Miguel a tattoo shows the level of interpretation and reflection inherent in the practice as well as the broad community of practice that is connected to the meaning behind the tattoo.

In the last of these three chapters, "Scratching, Cutting, and Juggling: The Turntablist as 21st-Century Scholar," I show the complex practice of making connections between disparate sources through turntablism. Gil's personal history with the practice reveals the importance of a community of practice through which Gil acquires material culture and a language. I then take the reader through several spaces connected to Gil's turntablism. I begin this journey with two significant and expected turntable spaces—the record store and a music room—emphasizing how they supply important performance spaces where Gil can develop an argot and an aesthetic within his craft, and where his community of practice can congregate and inform each other's work. I then move to a recording studio where Gil and an acquaintance experiment together and reflect on that experience. The chapter concludes with a discussion of the turntable work Gil does in his bedroom. In this case, Gil uses his turntables to interpret and reinterpret speeches by Martin Luther King Jr. and Malcolm X.

In the final chapter, "Teaching and Learning: A Shared Practice," one central question focuses the discussion: How can teachers teach in ways that embody the habits of mind and body that youth employ to get their work done? In order to answer this question, I suggest that teachers need to become ethnographers and amateurs. As ethnographers and amateurs, we can work to understand how our students are creative and intelligent human beings. I then discuss how performance, experimentation, communities of practice, evaluation, reflection, and interpretation can be the criteria for designing learning environments that are personally meaningful and rigorous for students and teachers. The chapter and book end with a call to design curricula as infrastructure. One way to do this, I contend, is to shape classroom learning around inquiry because of its natural parallels to the ways youth learn on their own terms.

In closing this introduction, I wish to avoid within this book any attempt to understand the youth work that I am exploring here as an attempt to get at *the* method for teaching and learning. In other words, I resist the idea of plugging these creative practices into the classroom in the form of discrete units of study or curricula. This form of integration rarely ever works. Making these kinds of practices units of study often ignores the fact that youth engage in this work outside of school and that they control the ways in which their work utilizes and is influenced by school. In this way, their work is not subject to the grading or disciplinary regimes of modern schooling (Aronowitz & Giroux, 1993; Foucault, 1995; McLaren, 1994). Here is another place where the distinction between the practice of the work and the products that the work generates is important. The marginal status of these creative practices—the fact that they are not appreciated in the mainstream—is what, in part, gives the practices power. The subversive nature of these art forms contributes to the interest youth have in them. A pedagogical stance where these practices are viewed as units of study, objects to be examined, takes this power away and can render the practices lifeless in the classroom. We need to avoid this at all costs. Instead, the objective of this book is for teachers, administrators, and parents to think about teaching, students, classrooms, and schools through the specific youth creative practices discussed. We do this by designing classrooms as *youthspaces* where the everyday creative practices of youth and the privileged competencies and conceptual understandings of school foster each other's development.

1

MULTIPLE WRITING (CON)TEXTS
The Writing Life of a Zine Maker

By early spring of 1999 when I researched Ian's creative practice of zine writing and spoken word, I could tell that certain things were not going well for him. In particular, he was having problems with school. His grades were falling and his parents as well as his teachers were concerned. I became aware of this slide in a few ways.

Around the first of March, Ian gave me a copy of his latest zine. This zine was a departure for him. He decided not to title it *The Antisocial*, the title he used for over a year. Instead of filling it with, in his words from the introduction of this zine, "social/political commentary through essays and pictures," he titled it *Harvey in the Well* and filled it with his poetry and a few administrative artifacts from school. In the introduction to this zine, signed at the bottom by Ian, he explained that he no longer felt the need to publish *The Antisocial*. Several of his friends were publishing zines and Ian wanted to "make something that was purely self expression." He ended this introduction by writing:

> It's easy to distribute a confrontational zine full of rants, interviews, and comics, many of which you are not even personally responsible for. It's easy to hide behind layers of images, behind cynicism and sarcasm, behind dogma and rhetoric, behind the ideal of giving everyone a chance to express their political views. It's quite another thing to stand naked.

One way in which he stood "naked" in this zine was to publish a progress report from his French teacher. He placed it in the middle of the zine: a photocopied reproduction of the progress report with the address of the school and the name of the teacher blotted out. The typed progress report read:

> Ian's most recent quiz has brought the written portion of his grade down from a C– to a D. Despite my suggestions to do so, Ian does not come to see me for extra help. I think it would help him to do some practice questions before he takes quizzes and tests. It would also help him to hand in a rough draft of a composition and to make an appointment with me to go over it before the final draft is due. However, Ian does not take the initiative to do these things. He is very quiet in class and I don't think he has asked a question all trimester.

When I read this, my initial reaction was anger and frustration. Here again, I thought, is a teacher who has absolutely no idea about the other work that Ian is doing outside of French class. I was also amused by the irony that the French teacher wished that Ian would do more than one draft of a piece of writing before handing it in. If only she had a glimpse into the complex drafting process through which Ian crafted the writing for his zines and his spoken word pieces. It seemed rather obvious to me that here was a case of a class that Ian just did not care about. And the teacher framed it as Ian's problem and not hers.

These feelings of mine were further fueled by another progress report that Ian included in this zine. This report, from the same trimester, was from his dance teacher. Ian had decided to take modern dance to fill his sports requirement at his school—a daring move for a young man, even at this fairly progressive institution. Ian placed this report on the page opposite his introduction. The dance teacher wrote this report in slanted cursive. It read:

> Ian came to me as, what we call in the business, a totally "raw" dancer. He had no technique, no concept of how to "count" in dance. His body defied him when he tried to make it execute a step. But he consistently worked at it and worked it until he conquered the challenge. I admire him for this. Needless to say, he learned all the steps and danced well in the show. "Way to go, Ian!"

At the core of this honest and critical review of Ian's work in dance is deserved praise for his steadfast effort to learn how to do something that this instructor intimates was almost unnatural to Ian at the beginning of the semester. Indeed, according to the teacher, Ian's own body rebelled against the effort at first. The contrast between these two progress reports is stark. Why, I thought, was Ian doing so poorly in French, a subject that

I knew he had excelled at in the past, and so well in a subject that was almost completely foreign to him at the beginning of the trimester?

With a few days' distance from my initial reading of the zine and these two progress reports, I could see that Ian's French teacher was legitimately concerned about Ian's work. The teacher wanted him to do well and was a bit frustrated by his seeming lack of interest. Ian and I had a chance to talk about this one day in the car on a drive down to the city. There were times when we would be driving around, and something about the journey would open up a space to talk about serious issues. On this drive, Ian shared his frustration with school. This of course was not the first time he had expressed his ennui regarding classes, but there was a different tone. Before, he would talk about classes in a sarcastic way, saying what a waste of time they were, but then also continued to do well in them. Now there was a tinge of exasperation in Ian's voice, almost as if he was not sure why he felt the way he did. He said, "I don't need to take the practice SATs. I'm going to take the real ones next year anyway." He complained that he did not feel like he had time to do his own work. He reiterated how inane he felt a lot of the work was for school. And he expressed consternation at many of his friends who seemed to just go through the motions of school, not thinking critically about what they were studying or why.

At one point on the drive down, I turned to Ian and said, "Can I talk to you as a friend for a sec?" He nodded. I told him that I was concerned about the way he was talking because I felt like he was allowing other people to control his education. I told him that I was afraid that if he "gave up," his educational choices in the future would be limited. The way I remember this drive, I do not think Ian said anything after my cautionary monologue. We just stared forward through the windshield as we passed the jagged granite cliffs on the side of I-76.

This conversation, and Ian's way of representing his present academic state, stayed with me over the course of that week, which ended, surprisingly, with a call from Ian's father. It was late at night. I was in the kitchen, putting the dinner dishes away. Ian's father and I had not talked much together up to this point in the research. He had asked a few questions about the research in the beginning, but most of my conversations were with Ian's mother. Ian explained to me that his father was incredibly busy with his job and travels often. So when I received the call from Ian's father, my interest piqued.

Ian's father called me from his office. He said that at this point, he did not want Ian to know that we had talked, but that he knew that Ian respected me a great deal and that he and I spent a lot of time together. I remained silent as he worked his way to the reason why he wanted to talk to me. He asked me if I had noticed anything unusual about Ian's behavior. I said, "No. Not really," even as I had our recent conversation and his zine and school in the back of my mind. Ian's father explained that both he and Ian's mother were concerned about Ian. His grades were falling precipitously, and he did not seem to be well physically. He was not getting much sleep. He also did not seem to care about the fact that he was not doing well in school.

While we were talking, my mind replayed the progress reports and Ian's and my conversation. I also thought about my own experience in high school. I thought about Ian and what was fair to him in terms of what I would share with his father. Did Ian tell me all of that stuff in the car in confidence? When I told him that I wanted to talk to him as a friend, did that change what was confidential and what was not? I was not sure what to say to his father so I told him about my own experience in high school. How, as a junior, I had burned out: "Used to go up to my room and just stare at the work"; "I didn't even know where to start"; "I went down an entire grade point in my average." "There were days," I chuckled, "when I would come home from school and flop onto my bed with my shoes on and take a two- to three-hour nap." I told him that my parents sent me to a psychologist, more than one, but it did not seem to help. I told him that the following year I found a reason to work again and made my way out of the slump.

I then reassured Ian's father that I cared deeply about Ian and wanted him to be successful. I would also never want Ian to hurt himself in any way, I stressed. Ian's father told me that they had set up a doctor's appointment for Ian. He added that Ian was comfortable with this doctor and had had many conversations with him in the past. He asked me if I would mind keeping an eye on Ian and letting them know if there was anything that concerned me. I told him that I would.

An ambivalent feeling swept over me when I hung up the phone that night. I felt as if I had been dishonest to Ian's father. At the same time, I felt as if I had to honor the trust between Ian and me. Finally, I was not sure how serious Ian's current educational or "psychological" state was. Granted, he was falling behind in certain classes, but I had done the same thing. It happens to many students and they bounce back, I thought. In my mind, I had no doubt that Ian could rebound, if he wanted to. But what complicated the issue the most for me was the enormous amount of work and learning I had witnessed Ian do over the course of that year in our research and how that did not seem to factor into our conversation at all.

This chapter focuses on the work in which Ian was engaged in the midst of the academic struggles outlined above. In particular, I discuss Ian's creative practice as a zine writer and spoken word artist over the course of a year. I begin by laying out a brief history of zine writing as a way of defining the art form. I move to showing how Ian became interested in zine writing and spoken word through the interrelation of experimentation and performance, and the community of practice he formed. I then show how his work evolved and changed over time in relation to the multiple aspects that contribute to the development of his creative practice. I do this by focusing on the evolution of one of Ian's poems: "We are the Sons of John Brown." Finally, I show how his performance of "We are the Sons of John Brown" pushed him into other spaces and performances that broadened his creative practice.

A BRIEF HISTORY OF ZINES AND ZINE WRITING

A zine is a handmade, amateur publication that focuses on a particular interest of the publisher. It differs from a newsletter or magazine, for example, because of its handmade nature. While some zine writers may use desktop publishing software to lay out their zine (often termed an e-zine), many literally get down on the ground and, with scissors and glue, cut and paste their zine together. Zine writers often distribute their zines free of charge, for a donation, or for a minimal fee (one or two dollars an issue). They then photocopy additional copies to distribute.

The audience, like the interest, is specific and limited. Generally publishers of zines make no more than 2,000 copies of each issue to distribute. Chepesiuk (1997) describes zines as having "offbeat, frequently provocative and often weird names, such as *Baby Fat, Diseased Pariah News*, and *Holy Titclamps*," the last title being a particular favorite of Ian's. Chepesiuk continues, "They lampoon, attack, parody, entertain, or instruct on virtually any imaginable aspect of our culture, from AIDS to poetry, dirt bikers, New Wave comics, and the popular television program *Beverly Hills 90210*" (1997, p. 168).

The zine, as Chu (1997) suggests, has its roots as deep as Martin Luther posting his "Ninety-Five Theses" on the Castle Church door at Wittenberg. However, Friedman, the publisher of *Factsheetfive*, a bimonthly review of zines, traces the history of zines back to two origins. He suggests that contemporary zines, like Ian's *The Antisocial*, are influenced by the Beat poetry of the 1940s and 1950s as well as by the pulp science fiction of the 1930s. Beat poets designed handmade chapbooks of their poems in order to distribute to interested readers. The pulp science fiction was primarily generated by sci-fi fans who would copy their own writing "commentary and manifestos" to friends and fellow fans of the genre (Gross, 1994). Both forms of media were produced outside of the legitimate publishing circuits of the time.

This underground publishing movement gained momentum in the 1970s with the explosion of punk music and punk culture. Music fans would publish zines based on whichever band they liked the most. Within these zines, the writers would also offer "general critiques of contemporary mores and aesthetics but always reflecting the personal tastes" of the publisher (Gross, 1994). These zines are often referred to as perzines (short for personal zines) because of the sometimes painfully personal nature of the content and the individual nature of the production and distribution.

The 1980s to early 1990s were considered to be the heyday of zines. According to some estimates, in 1992 there were over 20,000 zine titles published in the United States (Chepesiuk, 1997). Ian marked the early 1990s as a particularly rich time for zines:

> So much great zines came out especially in the '90s, you know? Not to hit on the whole zine revolution thing, but it's true…And a lot of them were unique and didn't have that sort of punk thing. I mean they obviously came out of punk in a way, but that wasn't necessarily their primary thing. And a lot of them were quirky and ironic.

Contemporary zines run the gamut from traditional fanzines that follow the careers of particular bands to travel zines that document the journeys of the writers to political zines that rant against the status quo. Many zines incorporate all three of these genres. However, according to Gunderloy and Goldberg (1990), most zines have a half-life of about two years. Often, a person will only publish one issue and then stop. Some writers publish zines incredibly sporadically—only one or two a year and at random times. Libraries interested in collecting these primary sources of mass culture become frustrated because publishers may change the name of their zine every issue, making it difficult to catalogue the material. Chepesiuk (1997) and Chu (1997) suggest that the elusive quality of zines is purposeful because the writers are not interested in mass media exposure. In fact, many zine writers will discontinue their zines when and if they garner mass media attention. Greta, the publisher of *Mudslap*, contends, "If you're mainstream, you can't steal postage. You can't plagiarize. You can't ditch bills. You can't be incendiary. You can't be yourself" (Gross, 1994).

Like turntablism and graffiti, zines are a certain type of youth phenomenon. Most are published by people under the age of 30 (Chu, 1997). Like graffiti, many publishers of zines use their publications to manipulate traditional uses of text and image in order to make provocative meanings. Many zine publishers abhor white space on the page and will fill it with everything and anything, giving many pages a pastiche feel. Some zines, like *Cometbus*, a zine with an incredibly long publishing life (over 20 years), and one of Ian's favorites, are nothing but text. Often, the text will "crawl off the page" (Gross, 1994); the words as icons create images and meanings. Zine writers also use the pages of their zines as a cross between a canvas and a piece of paper in order to manufacture their messages. Gunderloy writes that zines are places where "new languages are being invented and learned" (Gunderloy & Goldberg, 1990, p. 58). Lankshear and Knobel add, "Mainstream discourses and values are subverted and pilloried in ways that often are quite delicious" within zines (n.d., p. 4). Zine writers often interweave text with pictures in such a way that both "images" take on new meanings. Like graffiti, zine writers walk the fine line between recognition and obscurity. Zine writers veil their identities much like graffiti artists do, often using pseudonyms, and select their audiences carefully through personally delivering the product and constructing a message that includes a limited audience.

Chu contends that youth use zines in order to carve out their own space within this media-saturated world. This space enables zine writers to circumvent the commodified and controlling world of adult-run, hence mainstream, media. In a world of fewer and fewer independent media voices, coupled with the increasing surveillance of youth, zines, in her opinion, are one of the last places that youth have agency. She writes, "As much as they are critiques of mainstream media, zines also point to media as one of the last hopeful environments where young people can assert a sense of agency by redefining a social space in otherwise constraining material circumstances" (Chu, 1997, p. 82). I see agency in the handmade nature of these publications as well. Because writers like Ian literally sit on the floor and piece these works together, they often maintain a high level of originality not seen in mass-marketed publications.

As the publishers of *Central Park*, a zine out of New York City, included in their introduction, "We feel the world is in dangerous need of a new perspective, and we choose what we want to publish based on how it might contribute to such a perspective." From the 1930s to the present, zines as well as graffiti and turntablism have been spaces where youth control the production and distribution of ideas. In particular, Ian's zines are spaces where he wrestles with issues that affect him. Zines are a space where he finds new and refreshing ways to interpret these issues as well as represent how he wrestles with them. Ian's zines and spoken word pieces are spaces where he can challenge the ways in which mass media and many adults misrepresent what it means to be young and where one can see the multiple sources Ian draws on in order to make meaning through this creative practice. Finally, Ian's zines are spaces where he creates opportunities to learn "on his own terms."

BECOMING A ZINE WRITER AND SPOKEN WORD ARTIST

Months after the official data collecting ended, Ian and I e-mailed back and forth to one another one day. The conversation rambled, loosely focusing on the movies we had recently seen, the music we were listening to at the time, what he had been up to at school, and what he had been working on with his writing. Ian told me that he had applied and been accepted to the Governor's School for the Arts—a prestigious summer arts school. As part of the application process, Ian wrote an essay that told the story of how he became involved in zine writing and spoken word as well as why these forms of creative expression are so important to him:

> It's always seemed to me that creating was better than merely existing. I never wanted to just get by in life, to simply do well for myself. I've always wanted to create, to form something better than myself. I've always felt that for my life to be complete I would have to be able to create something worthwhile, and that these creations would be the manifestation of my life's purpose. When I was very young I wanted to be a scientist, because I believed them to be modern-day magicians who went around creating magical inventions. Later on I wanted to be a rock star because there was still magic in that. Eventually I discovered that language came much more naturally to me than music, that this was the medium I was meant to create with, and so I decided that I wanted to be a writer. My goal in applying to the Governor's School for the Arts is quite simple: to help myself to become a better writer.
>
> My first foray into writing was "The Man Who Stole My Woman Away." It was a tragic poem/song about an acrobat stealing the woman I loved, and was largely based on imagery stolen from old *Popeye* cartoons. For the next six or seven years I stumbled on in this manner, occasionally writing uninspired poems, and plinking away on a little acoustic guitar. The urge to create—and the knowledge that I someday truly would—was there, but in those days I was more concerned with making it through little league with the minimum amount of humiliation than with honing my craft. I was confident that I would someday get to be a producer of

culture, but for the moment was content (or at least resigned) to sitting in my room and consuming the work of others.

All of this changed when I was twelve years old and discovered punk rock. The power and sheer rage of punk rock was of course exciting. But more important to me than the actual aesthetic was the DIY (Do-It-Yourself) ethic of punk rock, the idea that you didn't have to rely on anyone to do what you wanted to do; you could make your own shirt, you could start your own band, you could publish your own zine. And so I did. I formed a band with a few friends, and was delegated the role of lead singer. Though my vocals were no sonic asset to the group, the chance to screech my (rapidly developing) poetry through a microphone and over some power chords gave me increased confidence and drive to continue my writing. I also began publishing zines. They started out as crude political pamphlets, but over a period of two or three years they developed into large, painstakingly crafted works featuring essays, rants, interviews, collages, and poetry. I am by no means finished with the medium, and am glad that I will always have this resource to feature and disseminate my latest project, whatever it may be.

In the past year or so I've begun to take my work in new directions. One of the most fulfilling things I've been involved in is spoken word poetry performances. I've been interested in the genre for many years, essentially from the moment I heard my mother playing cassette tapes of Jack Kerouac. I read a poem of mine at an open mic at the legendary Painted Bride Art Center in Old City, Philadelphia, and was warmly received by the audience. At his request I gave my number to the MC (who happened to be the Bride's poetry curator), and several months later received a call from him inviting me to join a collective of young Philadelphia (I'm the one suburban exception) poets. This has been a rewarding experience, and has given me the chance to meet some other up and coming writers, and to do some more performances. I enjoy the immediate relationship between the author and the audience in spoken word, and intend to continue performing my poetry every chance that I get.

My most common writing experience these days seems to be me sitting on a bench somewhere furiously scribbling in my notebook (constantly on hand), trying to write a better poem. Some times I like to think that I'm even succeeding. It's been a long journey so far, and I am clearly far from finished. In this essay I've focused on my output, but I certainly could not have done any of it without the inspiration of an enormous amount of books, records, and other art, as well as the help of some good friends, some nice strangers, and even some teachers and family members. I will continue to utilize these resources, as well as any other resources which I can get access to, especially one as wonderful as the Governor's School, in order to become a better writer, and to create more beautiful things than I ever have before.

This essay is an interesting glimpse into the trajectory of a youth's interest in a particular creative practice—from his initial foray to being an experienced practitioner. It involves experimenting in the particular art form with really no idea of where the tinkering may lead. It involves finding a community of practice. It involves experimenting with these other people on a regular basis. Ian developed an interest in writing through performing his work as well. And it is through publishing these zines that he refines his craft. The first few zines, according to Ian, are crude little pamphlets, but over time, and with further experience, the zines become more refined, more purposeful, more carefully done. The immersion into this particular kind of writing pushes him to look at other outlets as well. Both the publishing and the spoken word connect him with other people who influence his writing. These two writing activities and the community of practice that Ian speaks of also introduce him to a world of resources (writers, albums, movies, art) that Ian consumes, interprets, and filters into his creative output.

Ian describes in his essay to the Governor's School a group of people that share an interest in zine writing and spoken word. Through publishing together, reading together, and spending time together, they construct a particular understanding of zine writing and spoken word. They also define what the practice looks like in the everyday. Ian is connected to more than one community of practice. He considers himself to be a part of the punk scene and its various groups. He also identifies with the collective of young Philadelphia writers. Finally, he has assembled a community of practice through the collaborative nature of his zine writing. Part of what makes Ian's work with zine writing and spoken word possible is the way in which he sees how these various communities of practice intersect, share values, and inform one another.

Ian's evolution as a zine writer and spoken word artist begs the following questions: When are youth allowed to tinker in school? When are they allowed to slowly develop or find an interest in something? In academic classrooms, when are students given the opportunity to form communities of practice? When are they able to perform work that they are doing and see how their peers can actually inform and influence that work? When do teachers engage students in finding and making explicit the disparate resources that come together to help youth construct enduring understandings? Wiggins and McTighe write that an enduring understanding is one that uses "discrete facts or skills to focus on larger concepts, principles, or processes. They derive from and enable transfer: They are applicable to new situations within or beyond the subject" (2005, p. 129). I stress academic classrooms here because this kind of work does happen in schools outside of classroom spaces: in jazz bands, sports teams, debate clubs, etc. But we need to introduce Ian's way of working—a more natural way of developing a sustainable interest in something—in the classroom.

Ian's process of developing an interest in zine writing and spoken word resembles what science educators have advocated for quite some time: when designing learning environments, activity should always come before content. My experience working with these youth has shown me that the work that they do on their own terms always follows this pattern. They must immerse themselves in a particular kind of activity before they can even begin to see what it is that they need to learn, the skills and procedures that they need to develop, and the factual knowledge that they need to acquire. It is the immersion into the activity that generates the questions that lead youth to the content.

In what follows, I look more closely at how Ian immerses himself in these creative practices. I also examine the ideology behind the work and the specific activities in which he engages. Through further description of the ways in which Ian goes about doing the work of being a writer, we can more readily do the pedagogical work of translating these habits into the English classroom, for example. I will now move to a discussion of the DIY punk ethic that infuses every aspect of what Ian does within zine writing and spoken word.

DO-IT-YOURSELF: A CLOSE LOOK AT
THE ETHIC BEHIND IAN'S WORK

DIY (Do-It-Yourself) is an ideology, a way of being, that developed within the punk movement of the late 1970s. As Ian states in his essay, the DIY ethic is fairly self-explanatory. The artist is in complete control of the art. Everything from creating to distribution is solely within the hands of the artist. The theory is that if one is in control of the art from production to distribution, then no one else can control it, abuse it, or exploit it (Hebdige, 1979). The DIY movement of the late 1970s was in direct opposition to overproduced, corporate rock music at that time. Punk musicians wanted to wrestle music out of the hands of large record companies, thereby bringing music back to its roots—an art form with a political message and agenda.

This ethic appealed to Ian on many levels. For one, Ian saw similarities between the tension in music at the end of the 1970s and the present. The boy bands and top 40 bands that proliferated the airwaves embodied the corporate rock of today. Ian also saw that there was very little room for alternative voices to be heard not only within music but also within print media. In particular, youth voices within mainstream media, not to mention youth-produced printed media, were practically nonexistent. As a result, Ian argued, issues that effected youth were written from adult perspectives that often turned adolescent readers off. Ian started publishing his zine, *The Antisocial*, in order to create a space for his friends and him to interpret issues that adults often did not credit youth with considering—the Colombian civil war or the Mumia Abu-Jamal trial, for example.

However, Ian was not simply copying the zines produced within the first wave of the punk movement nor was he following a particular trend in the zines of today. Instead, Ian interpreted various forms of written and musical expression as well as his own careful criticism of current zine writing in order to craft his own message within his zine. By not sticking with one convention, Ian did not locate himself within a particular scene when it came to his work:

> I wasn't (and am still not) a part of a scene really, like I wasn't part of the Shreds or anything, but I was very interested in the punk rock/left wing activist movement, and had a few friends who were, so that was sort of a small scene I guess, in addition to the influence of the larger punk/activist scene...I've been trying over the past several zines...to have more in-depth essays with real sources, not just ramblings....I don't know how to describe my "culture," but mine has references...to various underground music, artists, politics, etc.

It was as if in order for Ian to become interested in the production of zines he had to align himself with particular communities of practice initially—in this case, the punk and left wing activist scene. But as his interest in zines and his own work in the medium matured, he realized that his initial identification constrained him and he needed to expand:

> I think what distinguishes me from a lot of over-political punk zines is the actual...references and context that I'm able to place things in, not ability necessarily, but I take the extra time to do. I

get the impression that a lot of people...I don't know even if they have the capacity to do it, they are interested in making a cool punk rock type thing that they can pass out at concerts. So they are not going to want to go through and quote people...but for me, I think I have the right balance that somebody like Sonic Youth [a band] has, where I have enough connection to punk that I can have the influence to do that kind of package like only someone with the DIY ethic would think to do, but that I'm not bound by that constriction.

Again, through the activity of writing zines, as well as a complex understanding of the genre and the ideology behind it, Ian's sophistication within the form increases as well. An essential component of doing the work is reflecting on his practice and evaluating the form. Through this critical lens, Ian comes to understand what he wants to do with the form and how his desires align with or deviate from more traditional kinds of zines. What is important to note here is that it is the connection to this ethic and the community of practice that perpetuates it that enables Ian to hone his practice and innovate. This identification with the beliefs, values, and practices of DIY culture more broadly, and zine writing more specifically, provides a learning experience through which he can react and establish his own, *unique* voice and aesthetic.

Later in the research, Ian commented directly on the connection between his work and the chapbooks, etc., from the 1950s, 1960s, and the present:

I hadn't thought about beat chapbooks in zine context, but now that i do it's absolutely appropriate...Another thing is the free press in the sixties, the underground newspapers...It's hard to think of good zines off the top of my head. I mean, there are good ones like crank [crank.com] or punk planet [punkplanet.com] that also come to mind, or like bust which started out as a zine but is more of a mag now, but these are all like fairly big established projects...But because of the nature of zines, sometimes the best ones are the ones you just pick up at a show or record store and maybe only 50 were made but you find a beautiful story in there...it's like, that's the power of them but also the frustration, it's so uncentralized, so unfiltered, so temporary...Sniffin Glue is the all time classic mebe, but I never seen it and i love the sky is burning cause i see the love germ [a friend] puts in ya know?... that's the nature of zines, if not a lot of this whole punk/indie/ whatever underground culture.

In order to construct his own understanding of what he would like to do in his zine, Ian, as the bricoleur, wove together groups of other practitioners composed of heroes from the music he listens to—Sonic Youth and other punk bands—as well as zine writers that he respected. Alexander Macgillivray (2002) defines bricolage as "the style of approach exemplified by a tinkerer or a jack of all trades. Bricoleurs are comfortable in unfamiliar realms of learning and experience because they learn best by using indirect connections to known information, even if the details of the skills are not exactly related. They try things out until they figure out how to do something." As a bricoleur, Ian blended these influences with historical movements in underground print media: free press in the 1960s, the small press movement, and independent publishers. Ian also identified with the content of several current zines that he found interesting.

Ian's understanding of himself as a zine writer was not a linear progression from one dimension to another. Instead, multiple sources influenced Ian at the same time, deepening his understanding of the historical significance of zines as well as the ideology behind the creative practice. These sources—the punk bands and the underground newspapers, for example—also referred to one another, reinforcing the importance and relevance of their contribution to the craft and messages of and in zine writing. Consequently, Ian informed his understanding of the form through reading and interpreting the content of other zines. It was through interpretation that he saw the connection between German existentialist literature from the 1930s and the current movement in zine writing. This reading also connected Ian to other sources and social relations through the World Wide Web. The zine writers that Ian followed often have Web sites that are connected to their print zines. These Web sites, in turn, also linked Ian to other Web sites that the zine writers felt were valuable. Often, Ian would communicate with zine practitioners via their Web sites or Instant Messenger on a regular basis. These conversations served to link the sources I mentioned above as well, showing Ian how the content of fellow zine writers' zines and the individual processes of their craft were informed by wide and varied cultural forms. As I mentioned above, Ian did not seek out this content or communities of practice in order to emulate or mimic the practice and product of other zine-writing practitioners. Instead, he interpreted the content of the work and the work processes of other zine writers critically, using them more as starting points for his own practice rather than as templates for his zine.

GETTING THE WORK DONE: THE
IMPORTANCE OF EXPERIMENTATION

Not surprisingly, there were no traditional classroom spaces where Ian could explicitly practice his craft. Much of this work happened outside of school. However, Ian did create space within school in order to experiment and perform his work. In this section, I highlight Ian's use and co-option of multiple spaces and time to experiment with his writing.

In English class in particular Ian often used the class time to edit writing that he was going to include in his next zine. He would not use class time to create new pieces but only to elaborate and craft working drafts. The creation of new pieces demanded a different, more personal space. When I asked him why he did not pay attention to what was going on in class, he assured me that he did, but that paying attention to class did not take all of his energy. At the same time, the content of the class was not terribly interesting to Ian. During one of our conversations about how the curriculum at school did not include many of the interests that Ian had, he expressed his frustration to me about English class:

Ian: This just blows my mind. Three acts into *Othello* a student asks the teacher if [Othello] is black. So part of this is that these are discussions that I don't want to be a part of. Or overanalysis of things. Just like going through things that I don't feel are worth talking about…I guess part of it is a personal thing. My shyness to go against the environment in an environment that doesn't expect me to go against it.…If the teacher asks a question in class, and even if I know the answer, if it's just a question from the book that anyone can answer, I'm not going to raise my hand and answer that. That's what I think 60% of classes at school are. That's a waste of my time, I think. So if we are just stating the obvious, I don't feel the need to state the obvious, and then if we are going past the obvious, we aren't necessarily going places that I really want to go. We just analyze the themes and then we boil down the themes to the Christ figure. Yeah, yeah, I just don't want to be speaking to that issue. I want to talk about why he chose the words he chose. Or this one thing, [the teacher] was like showing a scene, and it was pretty clear—this was in *The Things They Carried*—it was pretty clear that this image was of war. People were tearing it apart and looking for themes that weren't there and stuff. And then another student raises his hand and says, "I think that you are going too deep into

	this. I think we are supposed to just look at the scene and go 'Oh. He is just trying to show us the same feeling he's feeling.'" And then they start analyzing what the "Oh" means!
Leif:	What was the scene?
Ian:	I can't even remember.
Leif:	You know what story it was from?
Ian:	No. That's what happens. At the end of class, I don't even remember the story we read. I don't mean to be sounding like Holden Caulfield or anything, but…

Consequently, instead of suffering through these kinds of conversations, Ian redefined and reallocated class time to get work done that was meaningful to him.

Leif:	You said that you sit in classes and you just write?
Ian:	Yeah.
Leif:	Is that happening on a regular basis?
Ian:	Yeah. If I have something that I think I am going to work on anyways, I will use that as a time to work on it. But I won't just sit there and think of things. I noticed that there are other people that do this too.

Ian's manipulation of class time and space to serve his own writing is a nice illustration of De Certeau's concept of *la perruque*, "the wig." "The wig" is an instance when workers usurp on-the-job time to do personally meaningful work. De Certeau writes, "In the very place where the machine he must serve reigns supreme, he cunningly takes pleasure in finding a way to create gratuitous products whose sole purpose is to signify his own capabilities through his *work*" (1984, p. 25, his emphasis). In Ian's case, the machine was the predetermined/legislated work of the class. Here, Ian refused to allow the established order of the class to legislate what and how he should learn or write and at what time writing was appropriate. He was practicing an "ethics of tenacity." De Certeau explains that an ethics of tenacity is "countless ways of refusing to accord the established order the status of a law, a meaning, or a fatality" (p. 26). With De Certeau's notion of "the wig," the individual finds pleasure in subverting the expectations of those in power. Ian, on the other hand, was not "pulling one over" on the teacher. Instead, he reveled in the pleasure of having focused time and space to experiment with his writing. Ian was an opportunist, taking advantage of time to hone his skills as a writer and to write what he felt was personally meaningful material.

Ian's refusal to have his time disciplined was not a simple thumbing of his nose at the system. Through carving out this personal space within the public place of class, Ian found a focus that he did not have in other places, like his home, for example. In one of our many e-mail conversations, Ian explained to me how places like class as well as a Model United Nations conference created opportunities for him to write whereas when he had free time at home, he seldom took advantage of the time:

> During [Model United Nations] session I kept writing because they give you legal pads and pens which are what i love to write with, it was kind of boring and we had to sit still for hours at a time. I could focus like at school when i write, only more time and no one cared if I was paying attention. I mean, i didn't go to UN and write instead, but instead of sitting and listening or being bored i worked on stuff too.

Ian used the Model United Nations meetings to carve out another space for working on his writing. For me, this articulates Ian's sense of his need to have space and time for his work that coincided with purposes other than his writing. This juxtaposition of the intended purpose of a time and space (the lesson of an English class or the planned meeting for the Model United Nations, for example) with Ian's desire to work on his own writing made it possible for him to write. It provided the focus Ian needed to work. Consequently, if this juxtaposition did not exist (in other words, if Ian were left to his own devices), he probably would not have produced as much of his own writing. It was the act of appropriating this space and time and playing his own purposes alongside the intended purpose of that time and space that helped Ian generate his own ideas in writing.

In this same Model United Nations meeting, Ian created an opportunity to experiment and perform his writing and through that sharing reflect on its effectiveness. He writes:

> First i wrote some verse mocking stephanie...then I started writing serious rhymes, and revised them several times...i also wrote out the rough draft of my article on slam...I kept revising my verse and then i had two good little runs worked out and stephanie had apparently been reading over my shoulder and she attacked my rhyme pattern as being too simple just rhymes at the ends of line is basically what she said which is true...I realized rhymes are corrupting my ability to write poetry so i wrote a non rhyming poem which was alright.

Ian used the writing that he generated within that space to assemble a somewhat spontaneous community of practice that served to evaluate his work at that moment in time. It was interesting too that within this writing space and interaction with others, Ian moved from experimenting with words on the page to "writing serious rhymes, and revis[ing] them several times." Through this unique composing process, which involved writing in simultaneity with another activity and identifying others who were willing to experiment with him, Ian developed a critical perspective of his use of rhyming within his poetry. This community of practice pushed him to experiment with internal rhyme and through reflection on this criticism, Ian decided to write a free verse poem. In addition, these shared writing moments where Ian got to hear his own writing read aloud by others and praised helped Ian build off of the initial writing he did within that usurped space of legislated in-school time. What should also not be ignored is the element of play that is a part of this process. There is this quality of linguistic jousting going on between the *players* that keeps the activity interesting and challenging to the participants.

In addition, the acknowledgment of the act of writing as covert in this case was a stimulus for experimentation, evaluation, and production. In other words, Ian did not find all of the time in the Model United Nations meetings to be interesting and useful, and therefore, he took advantage of this downtime to do his own work. However, at the same time, there is a respect for the intended purpose of that time and space. Ian cared about Model United Nations and found it meaningful. That was why he was involved with the program in the first place. Therefore, it was not a simple matter of "rebelling against the system," for example.

This point opens interesting avenues for exploring why students have difficulty writing in English classes. It has been my experience that often teachers expect students to be working on a similar form of writing (an essay, for example), which addresses a text all students were expected to read, over a prescribed amount of time. This institutional process of writing does not in any way mirror or acknowledge the process of Ian's writing outlined above, nor does it recognize the idiosyncratic way in which Ian uses time and space in order to write. A 21st-century writing curriculum would recognize that the class is a community of practicing writers. This community would perform their writing with each other. This community would also, through working together, define what writing means to them. The members of the community would consider each other as writers, working on a craft. A 21st-century writing curriculum would also recognize the importance of experimenting when it comes to writing. Through playing with words, writing is fresh and intriguing, and the writer maintains an interest in it. A 21st-century writing curriculum would also honor the subversive nature of writing. Ironically, the writing should, in a way, challenge or subvert the doctrine of the classroom. A 21st-century writing curriculum would put into practice these spontaneous or immediate writing habits. They would use note writing as a way to push writing forward, for example. A 21st-century writing curriculum would understand that if students write in diverse ways on a consistent basis they will develop the skills of thinking critically about their writing and will be stronger writers in the end.

In the final chapter, I explore these ideas further, seeing how Ian as well as the other youth in this book, as creative practitioners, can help us think differently about how we teach writing, and how educational institutions can think differently about the way in which they conceptualize space and time in relation to learning.

THE STORY BEHIND "WE ARE THE SONS OF JOHN BROWN"

In the previous section, I highlighted the importance of Ian experimenting in and performing his writing in times and spaces organized for other purposes, positing that the cross-purposes, in part, help to energize his writing work. In order to more fully illustrate my theory of the interrelation of communities of practice, performance, interpretation, reflection, evaluation, and experimentation within creative practices, I now focus on the development of one of Ian's poems.

Ian used English class and Model United Nations as places to appropriate space and time to work on a poem that I feel is pivotal to Ian's development as a writer and spoken word artist: "We are the Sons of John Brown." The process of working on this poem connected him to other writers and performance spaces for his work that, in turn, influenced the content of his work and the evolution of his creative practice.

"We are the Sons of John Brown" took six months to write. Ian eventually published it in one of his zines and also performed it at an open mic, the first time he had ever performed one of his poems in public. He had put it aside for several months after the initial burst of work. Then, after he had attended an open mic and saw an advertisement for the monthly open mic at the Painted Bride, he pulled it back out again and worked on it intensively during "boring" classes. Ian explained the process of work necessary to perform the poem:

> I decided i wanted to do it when I went last week and it looked so cool...Last Sunday I was looking through some of my stuff, and i was thinking about the John Brown one, which was only the first stanza.

I realized it related to a few phrases or sentences i'd been kicking around, and wrote them all into one coherent thing that night. I had the paper with me pretty much the whole school week, going over it and revising it during boring classes, and so by like Thursday it was all polished and I had it pretty much memorized. but i kept going over it in my mind and out loud all Friday because i was afraid I would stumble or forget it. Abe's [a friend] great because he was willing to hear it over and over and reinforced my confidence.

Ian had used the open mic as a deadline for this poem. Ian spent months working sporadically on it, utilizing a boring class here and a boring class there. Whether or not he could take advantage of this time also depended on whether or not he had the work on him when he was in one of those boring classes. The writing of this poem, like the work for his zines, happened in spurts, until a few weeks before completion when the piece had so much forward momentum Ian could not do anything but put all of his effort into completing it. Notice also that an important part of the process of developing this piece for performance is the evaluative feedback that his friend, Abe, provided. Ian would not have even considered reading his work in public had he not attended a Word Wide Poetry event first and seen others performing their work.

The Painted Bride is a performance art space located in old city Philadelphia surrounded by converted factories and art galleries. It is distinguished by its fantastic glass mosaic entryway as well as by the avant-garde art that it features on a regular basis: everything from graffiti exhibits to the Sun Ra Arkestra.

At the time of the research, the Painted Bride held an open mic every first Friday of the month. Called Word Wide Friday, this event is emceed by Mark Lawrence, a rail-thin, iconoclastic, Beat poet who sports an assortment of porkpie hats and bowling shirts. When he is not emceeing Word Wide Friday events, Mark represents the city of Philadelphia with a team of poets in national slam competitions around the country.

Word Wide Friday is popular: so popular that the relatively small café space in which the event is held cannot contain all of the 300 or so people who buy the $6 tickets to get in. There are usually well over 20 people who sign up to read, and the performances can flow beyond 1 in the morning at times.

This particular night, the Bride, as regular patrons call it, was packed. Ursula Rucker was going to read. She had just recently been featured on the latest Roots album, *Things Fall Apart*. Being a Philadelphia native as well, it seemed as if everyone wanted to check her out.

I gave Ian and Abe a ride there. While we waited in line to buy our tickets, Ian noticed Mark Lawrence pull up in his car, and he said that he wanted to give him one of his zines. Ian had been to the Bride many times before this night. He had gone with his mother to see poetry readings. He had also gone with friends to other Word Wide Friday events. In a sense, Ian knew Mark Lawrence well. He had heard Mark perform some of his own poetry and appreciated his work. His desire to give Mark his latest zine was both a gesture of respect and a reaching out to another practitioner.

The first time he went out to give Mark his zine, Mark was talking to a group of people. I could see Ian through the glass doors, standing around for a while, hoping to take advantage of a lull in the conversation. Eventually, he came back inside and told Abe and me that Mark was too busy talking with other people. Ian kept an eye on him as we progressed in line, and when it looked like Mark really was not talking to anyone, Ian went back outside and introduced himself. It was a brief chat, during which Ian handed Mark his latest zine. When Ian came back in, he said that he was appreciative and asked him a little about the zine.

We found three seats together around the outer edge of the café space. The crowd was an alternative, bohemian group. Lots of black, gray, and muted colored clothes. Dreadlocks. People wore jackets with sayings on them: *Free Mumia*; *Anti-corporate America*; *Not for sale*. It was a largely African American audience. On the walls of the reading space were neon and digital works of art that pulsated and glowed. DJ Razor, the resident turntable artist, filled the air with beats mixed with sarcastic phrases he pulled from the records he played. Two video monitors were mounted above the left- and right-hand sides of the stage. They both showed spoken word artists reading at the Painted Bride and other places and various hip-hop artists' videos.

After sitting there for a while, Ian said that he was afraid that he was going to forget the poem. He did not want to read from the paper and had been practicing for days in order to remember it. I told him that maybe it was a good idea to use the paper so that he would not forget anything. I told him that being nervous was good. "It's good energy," I said. He smiled and then went back to going over the poem in his head.

Finally, Mark stepped up to the mic and gave a little introduction: "All right, all right? We have a special featured artist tonight, Ursula Rucker. Many of you know her stuff. She is going to bless the mic a bit later on." He paused for a minute, squinted in the intense light that illuminated the podium, and looked at the audience over his glasses. "As you all know, Word Wide Friday happens every first Friday of the month. We have been around for four years now. Our purpose is to highlight established as well as up-and-coming poets. Let's make sure that we support one another and it'll be a great night." He paused again. "Just to go over the rules: one poet, one poem. We don't want it to be too long if you know what I'm saying." He then squinted into the sheet of paper in his hand and read off the first name.

Before Mark called Ian's name, several other people got up to perform. After each person performed, Mark made it a point to reiterate a word or phrase that the poet used as a way of encouraging the audience to show their appreciation. At times, when one poet would "break it down," he or she would get instant approval from the audience in the form of claps, or laughs, or "whooo, go on!" Some of the performers would start off timidly and members of the audience would say, "Go on. You can do it." The pieces ranged from the hilarious to the deeply serious.

Then Mark introduced Ian. He stood up slowly and made his way to the mic. He resembled the three young men who went before him, except he wore a flannel shirt over a t-shirt. He had the same slow walk, the same mussed hair. I could even see the similarities in their eyes—dark and heavy. But that is where the similarity ended. Ian took the mic from Mark's hand and looked out over the audience. "This is the first time I have ever read in public," Ian quietly said. The crowd gave him a round of applause. He then launched into the first line of this poem, from memory:

We are the Sons of John Brown

We are the sons of John Brown
like the Daughters of the Confederacy
except that we were laughing when the Old South burned.
We are modern-day abolitionists
not exactly sure what it is that we wish to abolish
but we do know that we are pushing for a day
when America can be like South Africa.
Which is to say now that we have abolished segregation
let's free Mumia Abu-Jamal and make him president.
The good Reverend Jesse Jackson will set up a Truth and
  Reconciliation Commission
which will hold the FBI accountable for King's murder
and the Nation of Islam responsible for Malcolm's.
We are the sons of John Brown
because once upon a time they asked Malcolm if any whites
  could join him

and he said, "If John Brown were alive he could."
I would like to be thought of as someone who is righteous
  enough
that he could have hung with Malcolm—
wouldn't you?
We are the sons of John Brown
an entire subculture of self-hating crackers
who wake up every morning and look in the mirror
and wish that we could shed that pale sickly skin like a snake
who don't believe half of what they teach us in school
and are rightfully ashamed of the other half.
I'm not talking about some suburban minstrel
aping whatever he sees on MTV.
What I'm talking about is something different (I hope)
the kids who listen to Public Enemy
and write book reports on Nat Turner's confession
who know that the Black Panthers were real American
  heroes
and aren't afraid of affirmative action.
We are the sons of John Brown
and we're going to change the name of that show to
Donta Dawson's Creek.
In the first episode we're going to lock up Officer DiPasquale
so Donta can finally rest in peace.
In the second episode we're going to shoot David Duke
because it's about time somebody shot David Duke.
In the third episode we're going to try to build a world
where children are not judged by the color of their skin
or the price of their shoes
but by the merit of their character.
Then in the fourth episode we're going to have to face the
  inevitable white backlash.
The Christian Right will ascend to power
on a platform banning integration, immigration, sodomy,
  and not worshipping Jesus.
They'll burn this poem and all my zines
and brown-shirted Klansmen will drag us outside
line us up against the schoolhouse wall and shoot us.
But that's a risk that we have to take because
We are the sons of John Brown.
We are the sons of John Brown.

With that couplet at the end, the last line said even more loudly and forcefully than the first, the audience erupted in applause. People stood up with huge smiles on their faces. I spied several people looking at each other with expressions of amazement. People continued to clap and nod in agreement with the sentiment of Ian's poem. Ian quietly said thank you in the mic, handed it to Mark, and made his way back to his seat. As people turned and followed him with their eyes, some congratulated him and others just kept on clapping. Two younger women smiled at Ian as he sat down and told him that it was great. He smiled back at them.

During this prolonged applause, Mark stepped up to the mic, shook his head, and smiled broadly. "This is what it is all about," Mark said as the applause began to die down. "Up-and-coming poets reading their stuff alongside more seasoned poets." He paused for a minute to try to pick out Ian in the audience. "I expect to hear a lot more from poets like Ian." The audience voiced their agreement. Then Mark said, "Ian, make sure that you find me at the end of tonight so that I can get your phone number. I want you to come and read at [City High] where we do this program every month." He then turned back to the audience and told them about how he wanted to get together a young poets' collective that can represent Philadelphia in places like New York City and Washington, DC. With one more smile, Mark squinted down into the list of readers and announced the next poet.

When Ian sat back down, I tried to joke around with him about the response—my way of celebrating what happened—but he was not laughing at my jokes because he was still flying from this reading. Several minutes later, Ian took out a small pad and started writing down his name, address, and what he read for Mark.

The open mic continued for a good hour or so, and we stayed until the last minute. At the end of the reading, as everyone spilled out of the now hot and stuffy café, several people passed Ian and told him how great his poem was. A few younger women came up to him and talked with him about Mumia and prisons, and they asked him if he was interested in supporting National Mumia Day. He thanked them for the information, but his attention was mostly on Mark and giving him the sheet of paper with his contact information. He worked his way through the crowd leaving the café and eventually made it to the podium where Mark stood talking with some of the other poets. Mark said that he would be in touch with Ian soon so that they could talk about what might happen next.

A few days after this performance, Ian e-mailed me, reflecting on the event:

I was really nervous beforehand, but once I started talking I was at ease. Well not really at ease completely, i felt i knew what i was doing, but i was real eager to hear people react so i knew i was doing something good...not just at the end, but i mean reaction to specific lines. I was really pleased with the reaction i got...it was cool that so many people wanted to shake my hand or say stuff after the event.

This initial experience reading his work, and the conscious effort he made to connect with Mark, encouraged Ian to create more opportunities to practice his craft with others. Here, again, the community of practice that Ian formed within his zine writing and spoken word was crucial to the development and trajectory of his craft. Ian also used the reading as a source for evaluation of his work. He consciously decided to perform this piece in part to get a sense of the effectiveness of specific lines in the poem.

Fueled by the overwhelmingly positive response to "We are the Sons of John Brown," Ian decided that he wanted to read in the poetry slam that the Painted Bride was sponsoring for Word Wide Friday the following month. This time, Ian's reading and the reaction to his reading were quite different. The scene was fairly similar. The only difference was that this open mic was a slam, meaning that a panel of five people from the audience would judge everyone who chose to participate. The person who received the most points for his or her poem would win $100.

Once again, I drove Ian down with Abe. I asked Ian if he was going to read anything. He said that he was. He had just come up with the last line when he was buying his ticket. He was not sure how it would be received. He said that he had been thinking about the idea for a while. I asked if I could see it and he showed it to me. It was written down in a notebook. A paragraph or so of an essay for *The Things They Carried* filled the first third of the college-ruled page, and Ian had covered any other conceivable white space with jottings for his poem. He said that he was not going to read it, but then he had recited it in front of Abe and his sister and they both liked it. Ian added, "They could have just been nice."

At this reading Ian read at about 12:30 a.m., much later than the time before. By this time, Mark had left the stage and a woman had taken over the role of introducing readers. She read the names quickly like she was taking attendance rather than introducing readers. People were getting up and walking out when Ian took the mic before the woman who mangled his name could even step away. He looked out over the crowd and immediately sprang into this poem, literally throwing his body forward with the first line:

Paranoid Jewish Verse

They let a half kike up on the mic
And I'm like a Vietnam vet
Cause I can't forget
A long ago event
I call this Weisenthal disease
Some say collective memories
Holocaust fantasies
Do all Jews have these
Nightmares which got me so scared
I felt as if I was there
See Jews laying on the floor of the chamber
Like one once lay in the manger
You see I've been programmed
With fear of the Master Plan
Everywhere I turn I see the Klan
Not paranoid hallucinations
But real life evil Caucasians
Like Pat Buchanan and the Aryan Nations
And every time I see a cop, yo
I think about the Gestapo
Though I've never been beat by the PD
I always felt that they'd come for me
Because of speech that ain't free
Or possibly my ethnicity.

This time, his body moved with the cadence of the lines. He gesticulated with his free hand for emphasis, cutting through the air on the rhymes. Throughout the poem, people in groups of twos and threes filed out of the café, not seeming to pay attention to Ian. He faltered a few times. It looked to me like he was trying to remember the lines and then quickly found his momentum again. About halfway through the poem he dropped the mic with a loud thump. Some people applauded at this point. Ian picked the mic up again and launched into the last four lines. Someone laughed. With the last line, Ian immediately put the mic down and walked back to his seat. The woman came up and said matter of factly, "Give a big hand to Ian." Some people applauded in the midst of others leaving. Abe said on the walk to the car that he got a score of 35.

This poem came from a different place than "We are the Sons of John Brown." The clipped lines and the attention to rhyme were something new to Ian. He mentioned that in a later conversation we had about that night:

Ian: I shouldn't have read because I didn't have an ending. The second half of it didn't work…I just couldn't miss the opportunity…I think I did all right. And the time wasn't perfect either. Everyone was gone. Another thing is it's a style that pretty much everyone was using so having an original style would have been a good thing…I knew what I was trying to say, but I didn't articulate it very well.

Leif: What were you trying to say?

Ian: It's like these people that I know that always want to talk about the Holocaust and all the bad things, but there is stuff going on everywhere but they don't want to talk about it. That is what I was trying to say.

Leif: You went up there and performed something that you weren't sure about. Right?

Ian: Yeah.

Leif: You went up there and how did that feel?

Ian: Bad [laughing]. 'Cause like ["We are the Sons of John Brown"], I had worked over and over and I knew it was perfect. Parts of it I had been working on for months. And the thing with grabbing the mic immediately, I saw people were leaving and I thought they weren't paying attention so I was just trying to grab attention so that's why I did it so quickly.

Leif: Are you going to try to write in this form anymore?

Ian: I don't know. I want to rewrite this poem because the second stanza isn't good and I don't want to just leave it. I don't want to get caught up in it too much though because I think it can be helpful for emphasis and stuff, but you can get too obsessed with it.

Leif: So you are going to rewrite it.

Ian: Yeah. I don't know when I'll get around to it but I have to rewrite it sometime, at least the second half.

The performance of "We are the Sons of John Brown" encouraged Ian to read again in front of an audience, even if what he had was not entirely ready for public consumption. Witnessing others perform their work also gave Ian permission to experiment with the style of the second poem. He chose to write "Paranoid Jewish Verse" using end rhymes—a more traditional spoken word convention. While both performances gave Ian a comparative sense of where his work fits in with other practitioners, the differing responses to his work served differing purposes for his creative practice. The favorable response to "We are the Sons of John Brown" hooked Ian into a community of practice. It authorized the work that he was doing. Ian used this acceptance to muster the courage to perform the second poem. The lukewarm response to the second poem, maybe even the air of disaffection, prodded Ian to evaluate his work more critically. In particular, it encouraged Ian to reflect specifically on the style of the poem and whether that style was true to his own voice: "having an original style would have been a good thing." Rather than looking at the second reading as a failure, Ian saw it as an opportunity for evaluative feedback and planned to rewrite the poem, particularly the second stanza, when he got the chance. I wonder if Ian would have felt the need to rewrite the poem had he not read it in front of the Painted Bride audience. Would he have been able to "hear" the dissonance between the voice of "We are the Sons of John Brown" and "Paranoid Jewish Verse"? Would he have felt it a duty to rewrite the second stanza?

The Painted Bride audience served as a reference group for Ian. Their response, as well as how his poem compared to others, provided a context within which he could gauge the value of his own work. It also provided an opportunity to hear himself read the poem aloud. The intensity of a performance situation coupled with a working draft of a poem provided a space for Ian to look at and listen critically to his own work. He had read it to his friends and received what he construed as faint praise. So he found another community that he thought could evaluate his work more honestly.

The journey of "We are the Sons of John Brown," thus far, is a powerful demonstration of how communities of practice, experimentation, and evaluation interrelate in the poem's composition. The poem began as a scribble in one of Ian's many notepads of which he speaks in his essay at the beginning of this chapter. He came back to this scribble off and on over a period of months. Then, about a week before the first time he performed it, he uncovered it when he was rummaging through some of his work in his room. From this scribble, Ian used classes and Model United Nations space and time to elaborate and craft it. He also practiced the poem "over and over" in his mind as well as with Abe. After considerable work on the poem, Ian moved it to another space in order to perform it: the Painted Bride. Here, because of his performance, he was introduced to a new community of practice that had the potential to influence his craft. The overwhelming positive result of this experience convinced Ian to perform another poem in which he experimented with a style different from "We are the Sons of John Brown," a style obviously influenced by the other work that he heard at the Bride. Even though this second poem was not as well received, it provided a space for Ian to reflect on the content and rhetorical choices of his poem. Consequently, this performance served as a part of the process rather than as the culmination of the poem. As Ian stated, after performing "Paranoid Jewish Verse," he had a clear sense of the revisions that he wanted to make.

The journey and impact of "We are the Sons of John Brown" on Ian's creative practice does not end there, however. The experience of performing both poems at the Bride and taking part in a poetry slam pushed him to consider creating his own poetry slam at his school.

PORTABLE BRIDE: FORMING COMMUNITIES OF PRACTICE IN SCHOOL

This next phase in the evolution of Ian's creative practice highlights the significance of school as a space for his work. Ian used the space and time of school in order to bring together other communities of practice to continue exploring his craft. By organizing a slam within school, Ian created an opportunity to see other practitioners at work as well as expose himself to the content of their poetry.

The week after Ian performed "Paranoid Jewish Verse," we met at a bookstore close to his house and he sketched out for me his plan for having a slam at his school.

Ian:	I was thinking about how cool [the slam at the Painted Bride] was. Then, I'm not sure how I made the connection, but I was thinking that things like senior showcase and coffee house are relatively simple and student run, and you could have a slam that way...I mentioned it to Abe and Iona, just people who I thought would be interested, and I got a relatively good response. I was talking to Iona and saying that it would be really easy for me to set up the slam myself, but as far as getting permission and that kind of stuff, that is not my high point, so she said, "Well, I can do that." She went to Mr. Linet who said that she should talk to Mr. Adams. She went to Mr. Adams and talked with him for a half an hour...I was actually thinking of using the cafeteria, but Mr. Adams said it would be easier if we just used [the auditorium]. So I have to figure out a Friday in February or something.
Leif:	Do you think the auditorium would be a good place to have it?
Ian:	On the one hand it has a really high stage, and there's the punk attitude of the short stage, but for a slam the whole point is really populist and speaking to the audience so I

thought sitting in the seats really divorced from the stage, I thought that wouldn't be the ideal thing. But then on the other hand it is a real concentrated place where there is focus on the person whereas if it was in the cafeteria, it's an open communal space and it's just like really everyday and stuff so there's drawbacks to it, but I think the meeting room is as good as any place. Also, it's really easy equipment wise, and that's why Mr. Adams suggested it because you don't have to put the PA and stuff in there. Mr. Adams said that we need to talk to Eric, he's the student council president. He has to set some stuff up for us to make sure that it all works.

Leif: How are you thinking of designing it? How are you going to get people to sign up?

Ian: First I want to talk to Eric, Del, and Gil. Because I was thinking of getting student council support, and I was thinking of having Gil on the side, like Razor Damon [the DJ at the Painted Bride]. I think that would get people interested. If you just say poetry, people just say "Whatever," but if there is a DJ there, people know what kind of thing it is. Also Del has a good reputation within the school as a rapper. I've never spoken to him before but I was thinking I could try to get him interested and have him go first so then because if people know that he is doing it, if he goes first and all and sets the mood, that will give it the kind of reputation I want. And then announce it in assembly and hang up flyers.

Leif: When do you want to have it?

Ian: I was thinking about 2:30 on a Friday because it doesn't have a reputation or anything, to try and get people to come out is kind of hard, but if it's right after school and people are usually around until 3:10 or 4:00, so if there are people around they are going to be more willing to go to it.

Leif: Are you thinking of emceeing it?

Ian: I was talking with Iona. You can't slam and emcee because you can be biased, but she was thinking I should read because she doesn't think there are that many people at our school who have that many dynamic poems and will be able to give a dynamic performance so to get people to be able to keep up the level that you want for it...I think she doesn't have enough faith in how many people at our school can do stuff, and I'm not sure that if I let someone else emcee that it will get done right. I was thinking of having Abe be the scorekeeper because he can add things up in his head much faster than anyone else I know.

Leif:	Do you think that [the school] has any idea what a slam is?
Ian:	No. The people that I have been talking to are excited about it, but they really don't know what it is. Even Iona, she didn't know what the rules were or anything.
Leif:	Are you going to have a prize?
Ian:	I wasn't really sure what to do with the prize because I really don't want to charge because I think it is more important to have a big audience than to get money but obviously you need some incentive...I wasn't sure if the title would be enough—the title of being slam king or slam queen. I was thinking of "Supreme Lyricist" or something like that. My other main concern was how to have the sign-ups because if you have them too far beforehand it really takes away from it. So I was thinking that another good reason to get Gil is that I say that it starts at 2:30 and then it may not get started until 2:45 because if you have Gil playing then I can just be like, "Here is the sheet. Sign up." Then people aren't going to mind being there if Gil is spinning. [Returning to the idea of being emcee] The emcee is a part of the energy. I don't know if I can do that but I don't know if I can trust anyone else to do it.
Leif:	Why don't you know whether or not you can do it?
Ian:	I'm fairly articulate when I can sit back and revise something but just on the spur of the moment, I'm not the greatest at getting up in front of people and entertaining them...But like I said, I don't think anyone else knows what I am trying to do here.

In order to make this event happen, Ian wove his punk influence with the recent experiences he had at the Painted Bride. Ian's immersion into the global punk community—through his Internet connections with other practicing punks, extensive punk record collection, and experiences at punk shows—impressed on him the need for intimacy in terms of the performance space, a short stage that would bring the performer and audience closer together.

Ian imagined a group of people with diverse talents coming together to share their work, and in the act of performing their work, encouraging everyone to continue doing what they were doing. By creating this slam, Ian had the opportunity to form a new community of practice, composed of many people whom Ian did not associate with on a regular basis. The process of community building seemed to begin with a core of his friends—Iona and Abe, for example—and then this core went out and talked with the necessary people in order to make the event happen. Performance spaces like this slam allowed Ian to evaluate his strengths and weaknesses and rely on others to perform essential tasks. These spaces also made it possible for Ian to experiment—being the emcee for the event, for example, and going up to people cold in order to ask them to be a part of the slam. As a teacher, I am impressed by the level of reflective and strategic thinking involved in putting on this slam. Putting on this event required sophisticated planning: who to talk to in order to be able to put the slam on, who to invite to attract an audience, what day to run the slam, what roles certain people should play in order to have the slam run smoothly. The commitment inherent in the performance aspect of the slam requires this level of sophisticated, reflective work.

Two months after our first conversation about the slam, when Ian imagined the event, it happened. I arrived on campus at around 2:30 p.m., right in the midst of the mass exodus at the end of a school day. Students made their way out to cars, waited around for their bus, or just hung out with friends before heading home. The teacher on traffic duty directed me to a parking space. I then managed to worm my way through the clump of bus-bound students and into the foyer of the auditorium. Inside, students were hanging out in the cafeteria, sitting on tables and chairs. Others sat along the walls of the foyer chatting.

Opening the doors to the meeting room, I saw the rows and rows of benches, reminiscent of a Quaker meetinghouse, though more modern. There was a balcony of seats as well. The angle and positioning of the benches led my eyes up to the stage in front of the meeting room. This stage served as the space for dramatic performances, seasonal music concerts, weekly meetings, and open house introductions among other things: a platform for the arts as well as administrative duties. The stage was a space for performances of *A Midsummer Night's Dream* as well as for the dean of faculty to address the upper school student body regarding why a student was expelled.

The meeting room was a flurry of activity. Students hung out in the back of the room, sometimes sitting on the benches, sometimes milling around. Others ran up and down the aisles, jumping over the benches. The door constantly opened and closed as students poked their heads in to see what was going on, entered the room, or left. During all this commotion, Ian sat up front, a yellow legal pad in hand, looking a bit overwhelmed. I asked him how it was going and he said, "I don't know what is going on," half smiling. There was a sports awards banquet happening at that moment and other people had team practice, he explained. He was not sure if anyone was going to show up. While we had this conversation, Gil set up his turntables onstage. He positioned his turntables stage right. Sam, another acquaintance of Ian's and Gil's, came in not long after and started playing with Gil, laying down an original beat constructed out of beats he found on the record he was spinning. Gil punctuated Sam's beat with choice phrases he found on other albums. As these two worked side by side, a small group of Ian's friends stood directly offstage left, trying to figure out how to work the digital video camera.

Somebody came out from backstage and told Ian that the "drama lady was mad." The drama lady, aka Barbara, came out almost on cue and asked Ian, over the music, "Do you have permission to do this?" Looking tentative and running his fingers through his hair, Ian told Barbara that he had talked with Eric, the student council president, and he said that everything was all right. Ian also said that he had talked with Mr. Adams, the dean of students, as well. Barbara said, over the din of the music, "You have to come and talk to me in order to schedule the room." Ian apologized. She said it was not his fault. They had a rehearsal today and would have to find someplace else to do it. She also asked him if he had teacher support. Ian shook his head no. Barbara smiled, put her hands together, and said, "You need to have teacher support for this kind of thing, Ian." Ian nodded. Once they finished their conversation, Ian frantically ran out of the auditorium. A few minutes later, he came back and told Barbara that he found an English teacher to come in and advise.

During the time between sign-up and slam—about 20 minutes—Ian walked back and forth, either convening with his friends to talk about how to get started or how to get people to sign up. They sat in a huddle on the right-hand side of the stage, where a friend of Ian's was still trying to figure out how to set up the video camera.

Students were running around the space. Others hung out with Sam onstage. Some were breakdancing behind the turntables. Another friend of Ian's set up his tape recorder on the edge of the stage in order to record the event. Others came in and sat down and talked. At one point, I asked Ian if I could help. He said no, but told me that they only had 10 people who signed up. I asked him if he had thought of making an announcement over the microphone to get more people to sign up. He looked surprised and said, "Good idea!"

Ian walked up to the mic, asked Sam to turn the music down, and then uncertainly announced, "If anyone wants to read, the sign-up sheet is down on the podium. We're going to get started in a few minutes." A few students made their way up to the podium to sign up.

The slam lasted about 1 hour and 15 minutes. During that time, no adults or authority figures had to come in and redirect the energy. The English teacher that Ian ran to get sat in the back of the meeting room the whole time, enjoying the show. It was completely youth led, without much structure supplied by Ian. While he did lay down the ground rules for the slam—no props, no beats—the rest of the organization or structure seemed to come from the spoken word and poetry. There were also the five judges who supplied structure. But there seemed to be an understanding shared by the people there as to why and how this event was happening. This was evident by the supportive clapping and cheering as well as people telling others to be quiet while someone performed.

During the event, Ian played a subdued Mark Lawrence, announcing the next reader and every now and then throwing in a little something from the poem just performed in order to elicit more of an encouraging response from the crowd of about 50 students. Ian would introduce each poet and that poet would come down in front of the stage to the sound of cheers from his or her peers. Ian would hand him or her the mic, and the space, so to speak, would be his or hers. One person came up and made strange noises on the mic. Another young woman sang about her love for God. One guy channeled Henry Rollins, strolling back and forth on the stage like a caged animal.

One young woman's poem ended with the lines "In the confines of my own community / as I rediscover my constant internal beauty." The second to last line struck a chord as I sat with all the youth in the audience who applauded and yelled at the end of this poem. The line triggered a memory of a conversation I had with Ian several days earlier, when he told me a story of walking from the cafeteria to the upper school building. On the way, he overheard two students who were planning their Friday afternoon. One of the students shouted to the other that she was going to the slam. Here was a student Ian had never met, planning on going to an event that he had constructed.

These two lines helped me understand how important this slam was to this community. It is not surprising that the majority of students with whom I spoke that day explained that they never read their out-of-school writing in class, and that opportunities to even write "creatively" were at a premium. Teachers often leave creative writing out of their curricula because of the difficulty they perceive in employing traditional forms of grading as a way of gauging the worth of a "subjective" form of writing. Yet, it seemed imperative that spaces like this slam needed to occur in order for youth like this poet to "rediscover [her] constant, internal beauty." I also find it interesting that she used this slam to share a piece of writing that was a "work in progress." She read an unfinished piece to gauge an audience's response.

Another poem that stuck out for me was performed by Sam, the turntablist. His poem, bitingly sarcastic and funny, captured the energy of surrealism and the avant-garde. The unabashed humor and rather risky exploration of gender and sexuality made me wonder if the audience of students would ever read a poem like this in English class. Here is a short passage from the longer poem:

> I imagine a little cartoon playing in her head
> On a loop.
> In it: 2 sassy apes put bows in each other's hair, while Mr. X
>   and Mr. Y and
> Dr. X
> play reverse hopscotch.
> That is, they move down from six, to zero, trying to figure
>   out the
> number of chromosomes she should have—
> They keep stopping at 3, and
> I think they're trying to hint at
> something.
> "No," she says, "I have three already—and something is
>   wrong."
> This often confuses the people around her.
> —when she's ordering sheets and swimwear from Lands End
> —being ogled at by boys in Albany, NY
> —when she's pledging 165 dollars to PBS in exchange for the
>   Eastenders tie
> and matching lapel pins

What does a poem like Sam's do for other writers? What does this kind of exchange open up or allow to happen in future work? To begin with, one cannot discount the importance of Ian having the opportunity to hear and see his peers engaged in a similar kind of work—a physical manifestation of his community of practice. Sam's poem, it is safe to say, differs greatly from most of what Ian and his peers read in English classes. Creating a space like this slam enabled Ian not only to hear other kinds of writing but also to witness the favorable evaluation that that kind of writing can receive, a validation of sorts.

At the end, Ian was reservedly ecstatic. His eyes were wide and bright. He thought it went well and that if they did it again, it would be even better.

CONCLUSION

A week before Ian sent me his application essay for acceptance into the Governor's School, and a year after he had orchestrated the slam above, Ian sent me another e-mail:

> I'm leaving for Illinois tomorrow morning, i'll be gone for a week, then i'll be back for a few weeks before Governor's School. i'm sorry i haven't really responded to the chapters you sent (i have read them)...I'll definitely respond to all this when i get back, and maybe we can talk then.
>
> One of the things that has been making things hectic is that I've had to go to a lot of doctors and shit. So apparently I've had severe ADD all this time and no one noticed. This explains a lot of things actually such as the inability to deal with school work, the circular depressions, the random thought associations and loss of interest and stuff in the middle of conversations...a lot of shit. So starting today i'm on Ritalin, we'll see how this works out.

I had not anticipated Ian's diagnosis of attention-deficit disorder. Even after the conversations we had, the idea of ADD or Ian on Ritalin never crossed my mind. I had spent a year with Ian, witnessing him do an enormous amount of work, be productive, and learn a great deal. Before this diagnosis, Ian applied and had been accepted to the Governor's School. I knew that there were times when Ian was down or not being particularly productive, but I had interpreted that as the ebb and flow of creativity. I realize now that it was much more complicated than that. Yes, Ian did a lot of work, but he was not doing a lot of schoolwork, and that made all of the difference.

I wonder if Ian had stopped writing his zines or ceased to be interested in spoken word, if the idea of medicating him for this lack of interest would have come up. On one level Ian's e-mail brings to light, once again, what kind of work and learning is valued, to the point where when Ian is not doing the valued kind of work it becomes a medical issue. That said, I do not want to rule out or not honor the distinct possibility that the numerous doctors' diagnoses are accurate and that Ian will feel better about himself and do better in school because of the Ritalin. Within the e-mail, Ian sounds relieved that many of the feelings he has had can be explained. There is a "rational" reason for his "erratic" behavior. However, it makes me wonder what the medication is truly for. Is the diagnosis and subsequent medication designed to liberate Ian as a learner, or is it a way to mold Ian into the kind of learner that the rather constraining parameters of school needs in order to perpetuate its style of learning?

As I write this question, I know that I expose myself to criticism for possibly making an incredibly complex issue far too simple. That is not my intention. The questions are large and quite complicated. One of this book's intentions is to make the case that these kinds of creative practices complicate the notion of either being in or out of school and challenging traditional conceptions of what work and learning should look and feel like. By doing this, I hope to open a space to think critically about how pedagogy and learning environments in schools are often constructed in ways that privilege certain ways of working and exclude many others. Therefore, I think it is important to raise tough questions like the ones above.

In this chapter, I have articulated how communities of practice, performance, evaluation, reflection, and interpretation work together to help shape particular poems as well as push Ian's practice in new directions. Ian's process of working on his zines and spoken word pieces was sporadic. There were ebbs and flows to his work. At times his zines and spoken word writing took a backseat to other priorities. At other times, Ian's writing took precedence over everything else, including sleep. These ebbs and flows were influenced by many forces: one was school and the demand that it placed on his time. Because of this demand, Ian appropriated time and space designated for other learning purposes in order to do his writing. This appropriation involved more than resistance to the prescribed intention of that space and time. Ian recognized in his practice the need for spaces like Model United Nations to help him focus on his writing. In addition, these spaces provided other opportunities for developing communities of practice to explore his writing. Ian's creative practice also involved other spaces and time outside of school. However, these performative acts were not the conclusion of a piece of his work, as I show through the evolution of "We are the Sons of John Brown." Instead, Ian used his performances at the Painted Bride, for example, to receive much-needed evaluation on his work, to form communities of practice in connection to his writing, to push him to experiment in form and content, and to open new prospects for exploring his creative practice. In fact, Ian used performance to share unpolished work like "Paranoid Jewish Verse." Therefore, the act of performing can be interpreted as yet another step in the process of refining a piece of writing.

While intentionally separating communities of practice, performance, evaluation, interpretation, and experimentation in relation to Ian's creative practice throughout this chapter, I am wary of the way it may compartmentalize or cast them as unrelated instruments in their association with Ian's writing. Instead, I have argued through illustration and analysis that these aspects are interrelated. At times it was even difficult to distinguish them because of their dependence on one another to influence Ian's creative practice. The interrelation of these habits as means through which Ian produced personally meaningful writing provides a way into thinking about how we as teachers can approach writing in our classes specifically and in our schools more broadly. I will discuss this implication in the concluding chapter.

2

THE SHIFTING CREATIVE PRACTICES OF A PUERTO RICAN–AMERICAN YOUTH

Several months into the research, the three youth and I decided to get together and talk about their creative practices as a group. Miguel suggested we meet at his house. When we got to the bottom of the steps leading to Miguel's basement, Miguel pulled me aside among the clothes hanging next to the washer and dryer and said in a near whisper, "Yo, I ain't going to do graffiti no more." I paused for a minute, not completely surprised at his announcement. For a time I had expected Miguel to tell me something like this. Also, I had noticed that he had not been working on a new piece recently. Admittedly, my pause was filled with selfish thoughts: "What am I going to do now? Can I write this book with only two participants? Do I have enough about Miguel to be able to include him?" It is amazing how many selfish thoughts can go through one's mind when it feels as if the research is in jeopardy.

In the year and a half I spent with Miguel, I witnessed his slow move away from graffiti as his creative practice. Miguel's communities of practice, his interpretation of his life circumstances coupled with reflection, and the evaluative feedback he received from the police influenced Miguel's choice to at first find what he thought was a more "socially acceptable" representation for his graffiti. When this move did not work, Miguel began experimenting with other artistic forms such as building models, airbrushing his boots, and tying flies for fishing. By the end of the research, Miguel focused his creative practice on tattooing his skin. These choices and transitions did not happen quickly. It was a slow progression of events coupled with reflection, interpretation, and evaluation that convinced Miguel to modify his creative practice several times over the course of a year and a half.

Unlike Ian's zine writing practice, Miguel's practices of graffiti and tattooing are more socially problematic. Graffiti is considered illegal in the United States, and tattooing (particularly prison-style tattooing) is dangerous to Miguel's health. Because of the focus of this book—translating youth ways of working and learning into classroom teaching—I am not going to spend much time arguing for or against the practices of graffiti and tattooing. That is a topic for another book. Throughout this chapter, Miguel struggles with the illegality of graffiti and how his practice gets him arrested. Miguel also drops out of school. This decision is prompted by Miguel's unruly behavior at the school coupled with his feelings of being disrespected and boredom.

I do not want to diminish these aspects of Miguel's life. I also do not want to abdicate Miguel's responsibility within them. However, I do see them as secondary concerns in terms of the message of this book. I do not focus on the illegal or hazardous qualities of Miguel's chosen practices, for I am not really arguing for the worth or worthlessness of these practices. Instead, I want you to see the complexity of the work within these practices and to see the ways in which Miguel employs the habits of mind and body within them. I want you to take this approach because the influence of Miguel's practices for teaching does not come from the problematic nature of graffiti or tattooing. Rather, it comes from the way in which he works in them. In other words, what Miguel has to offer us as teachers is not an argument for supporting or advocating for graffiti or tattooing. Miguel offers us another compelling reason for seeing and treating students like him as young people with skills that can be utilized and further developed within classroom spaces. Perhaps through this perspective, we can design learning environments that help convince students like Miguel to stay in school, keeping in mind that it is not the illegal practice but the habits of mind and body that would be translated into classroom learning. Perhaps these kinds of learning environments can show students how they can work and learn on their own terms and that these can be assets in more socially acceptable practices.

In the last chapter I showed how Ian drew from multiple sources in order to inform his work, synthesizing various communities of practice and multiple forms of performance to receive essential feedback on his writing and to encourage him to experiment with form and voice. For Miguel, multiple sources and spaces served similar and different purposes. Miguel's entrance into being a graffiti artist was similar to Ian's beginning interest in zine writing and spoken word, as I will show.

However, the reasons for the shifts in Miguel's creative practice over time provide an interesting contrast from the supportive network and seemingly limitless access of Ian's practice. The obvious contrast is that graffiti is an illegal practice compared to either zine writing or spoken word, but this distinction only scratches the surface. As I will show, Miguel's engagement in multiple creative practices and his experience within these practices differ from Ian's case in complicated ways. Miguel's case provides an opportunity for examining how living in poverty influences the kinds of communities of practice that are formed, the way experimentation is used within a creative practice, what is interpreted and why, and the kinds of performances that take place.

In this chapter, I show the trajectory of Miguel's creative practice by first explaining his introduction to the practice of graffiti. I then discuss the development of his craft as a graffiti writer, arguing that the interplay of communities of practice (namely graffiti heroes) and the interpretation of various styles of graffiti mediate the development of this particular creative practice. Next, I show how other communities of practice—in the form of institutions like the juvenile justice system, school, and an organization for "at risk" youth, as well as the role of space to write and see other writers' work—contribute to Miguel's move to represent his graffiti on canvas. In order to stay true to the movement of Miguel's practice over time, I then explain Miguel's move away from practicing any form of graffiti to discreet one-off experiments (drawings for family, designing his room, models, remodeling homes, and repairing cars), showing the influence of familial obligations and lack of space to practice graffiti. Finally, the chapter ends where the research ended: Miguel's shift to tattooing his skin. Through an extensive vignette, I show the process of work involved in this creative practice. There is the interrelation of a community of practice and the interpretation of an art form through various media sources that influence Carlos's and Miguel's choice of tattoos. This practice also involves Miguel reflecting on his life circumstances. It is these life circumstances that made tattooing his skin, at that point in time, the only creative practice that he had the space and time to refine and shape.

A BRIEF HISTORY OF GRAFFITI WRITING

One of the four elements of hip-hop (the other three being rap, break dancing, and turntablism), graffiti has a long and dubious history in America. For the purposes of this book, I limit the sociohistoric roots of graffiti to the piecing of trains in the late 1970s to the mid-1980s in New York City because it is the history with which Miguel most identifies.

Graffiti involves the use of letters and words, among other textual representations, to construct meanings. There are different forms of graffiti that writers use for different discourse purposes. Generally, writers separate their graffiti into three types: tags, throw-ups, and pieces.

Tags are the names quickly scribbled on walls and other public spaces. They are written either with spray paint or markers. A graffiti writer primarily uses tags to get his or her name "up." The more a writer is seen the more he or she gets "rep" (short for reputation). Similarly, a writer gets "rep" by the number of throw-ups he or she is able to do as well. A throw-up is generally a three-letter nickname that a writer paints in bubble letters. These bubble letters are all in one color and then outlined in a darker color. Writers do not judge other writers' throw-ups on style. Writers judge other writers by the amount of throw-ups a writer does or by the amount of times a writer "gets up" (Castleman, 1982; Phillips, 1999). Finally, pieces (short for masterpieces) are large, intricately drawn works that often fill a wall or the side of a subway car. Writers take their time drawing these and often work from sketches in their blackbooks, where they hold all of their ideas for past, present, and future pieces. Writers paint pieces in multiple colors. They may involve the name of the writer—what Miguel most often does—or messages of different kinds. A famous piece is the Merry Christmas winter scene that covered the side of a New York Transit subway car (Castleman, 1982). Sometimes pieces may not involve any writing at all, only pictures.

Graffiti is considered a crime. During the course of this research, there were many stories of police arresting youth for tagging—the quick writing of names on walls, benches, and street signs, for example. At the same time, graffiti had been co-opted by "the art community" and musicians and through this co-option been legitimated within these communities of practice.

Conquergood considers graffiti to be a "counterliteracy" because it "challenges…the 'textual power' that underwrites private ownership of property and the regulation, control, and policing of public space" (Conquergood, 1997, p. 354). Similarly, Ferrell argues that graffiti is in direct response to an urban environment that is "increasingly defined by the segregation and control of social space" (Ferrell, 1995, p. 78). In effect, according to Ferrell, graffiti writers reappropriate public space that is most often either confining or aesthetically insulting to youth. This is why youth most often "bomb" or write on stop signs and public-owned buildings as opposed to cars or houses.

Graffiti artists choose to make their points in writing on walls, railings, trains, and billboards so that all can see. Yet they make their point in ways that only certain people can read and understand. Therefore the writer is ever elusive and often unknown to those who would like to punish him or her for these acts. Much like zine writers hybridizing text and image in their zines, graffiti writers do the same thing. Graffiti is a counterliteracy as well because it upsets common conceptions of what reading and writing are, similar to the ways zine writers fuse text and image in political collages. In fact, at times, the distinction between text and image can become so blurred that it is difficult to discern the difference between them.

George writes, "Hip hop didn't start as a career move, but as a way of announcing one's existence" (1998, p. 14). In the late 1960s, youth gangs used graffiti to define territory and to get "rep." The more the youth gang tagged their names around the Bronx and beyond, the more people and rival gangs saw their name. The more people and rival gangs saw their name, the more recognition the gang received. This graffiti was rather simplistic. The youth would write their gang name in permanent magic marker or spray paint on walls, inside train cars, anywhere where others from their gang and rival gangs could see it. The idea was to get their names up as fast and as often as possible. One could see the Savage Skulls or the Black Spades tags, for example, almost everywhere one looked.

These tags had their own style. Castleman writes, "Early writers... did not seem to care much what their 'hits' [early term for tags] looked like as long as they got them up and people could read them" (1982, p. 53). The practice of graffiti soon moved beyond the quick tags of youth gangs of the Bronx in the early 1970s, partially because youth gang activity mysteriously declined and partially because of a group of new writers, not gang related, who took the art form to a new level.

The most famous writer of this time was TAKI 183, a Greek immigrant youth who gained notoriety far beyond the Bronx because of his oft-seen tag "TAKI 183." Taki commented on this recognition: "My name got noticed because it was wider then everyone else's. But even more important, I was writing in a different area than most people. My name could have been on every street corner in Brooklyn and I wouldn't have gotten the exposure I got from writing on the East Side" (Hager, 1984, p. 14). Taki did not write his name on the wall to align himself with a particular social group. He did it for a different kind of exposure. Taki wanted to get recognized as an individual.

Permanency and durability are important aspects of a graffiti writer's craft. A writer's reputation not only lasts through the act of getting his or her name up often. A reputation also lasts by how long particular pieces exist. The longer the pieces stay up, the more of a history they create for the writer.

Taki was not only recognized by other young men who started writing because of him, but the *New York Times* ran an article about him as well. Taki's notoriety also helped push graffiti as an art form beyond the simple and quick tagging of someone's name. Writers started considering the size and style of the letters as well. Castleman writes, "As hundreds of new writers emerged…new emphasis began to be placed on style, on 'making your name sing' among all those other names" (1982, p. 52).

When the use of graffiti moved beyond a gang territory marker, it also moved beyond a writer's neighborhood. Soon writers traveled all over the city and its boroughs. Some writers, like Taki, ventured north to Upstate New York in order to tag. Here again, the idea was to get your name up as much as possible, but there was also the identifying marker of where you came from, the street address on which you lived. Perhaps more important, for the purposes of this study, writers like Taki 183, Lee 163, and Tracy 168 started congregating together, talking about their writing, sharing trade secrets, and refining their craft. These communities of practice often formed in and around high schools because most of the writers were in high school when they started. Hager writes of Phase 2, a well-respected graffiti writer of this time:

> Phase 2 joined a large number of writers at DeWitt Clinton High School. One advantage to attending Clinton was the proximity of a Transit Authority storage yard across the street, where parked trains could be found any time of day or night. It wasn't unusual for Phase and the other writers to spend their lunch hour in the yard marking up trains. After school, the writers would gather in a nearby coffee shop. Whenever a bus pulled up outside, dozens of writers came pouring out of the coffee shop waving markers. By the time the bus pulled away, it would be drenched in freshly scrawled signatures. (Hager, 1984, p. 17)

Castleman (1982) describes three different kinds of writing groups that formed. Often, new writers, or "toys," would get together to experiment, usually drawing either on paper or on walls around their neighborhoods. These "toys" would also seek out an "open membership" group. One or two "master artists" usually led these groups, and it was from these two leaders that the toys sought apprenticeship. Finally, there were also master groups that consisted of only five or so highly experienced writers. These groups were closed to unseasoned writers. Often the group of four or five stayed together, writing for many years.

Like any art form, with the growing number of graffiti writers practicing their craft and talking about it with each other the art form evolved and changed. Writers like Barbara and Eva 62 enlarged their signatures even larger than Taki and involved more than one color. They, along with other writers at the time, invented the "throw-up." Cay 161 incorporated other symbols with his signature by drawing a crown over his tag. Soon writers used walls and the sides of trains as large canvases where they would draw elaborate pieces. The writer's name would still be central to the drawing; however, other images and other text would be involved as well. Writers would also pictorially manipulate their names so that an outsider would have a difficult time identifying who the tagger was. Hager quotes Tracy 168 as saying,

> The best year for graffiti was 1973. Styles were coming out. We got into this thing with colors. First it was two colors, then three colors, then four. Then it was the biggest piece, the widest. Then it was top-to-bottom, whole car, whole train. We worked on clouds and flames. We got into lettering. Everybody was trying to develop their own techniques. When I would go into a [train] yard, the first thing I'd do is look around and see who was good. That would be my objective. To burn the best writer in the yard. And I wouldn't leave until I did something better than him. I put a Yosemite Sam with two guns on a piece. That was the first cartoon character. (Hager, 1984, p. 22)

These informal communities of practice in the 1970s evolved into official writing groups. Most of these groups were not gang related; however, rivalry between different writing groups was fierce and sometimes escalated into violence. Writing groups like the Mad Bombers, Wild Style, and Crazy 5 were prominent at this time. While these communities were insular and somewhat exclusive, writers could be involved in more than one writing group. The borders were permeable.

Inevitably, audiences outside of the graffiti writers began to appreciate their work. Newspaper and magazine writers published short articles on a particular writer or on graffiti in general. Then art dealers and others in the art world took notice, and graffiti found its way into the art galleries and onto the walls of clubs around New York City. Graffiti artists at this time no longer worked on concrete walls, but worked on the "sanctioned" media of the established art world—canvas. At one point, several graffiti writers were invited to Italy for a show of their work. Graffiti sold for $1,000 or $3,000 apiece. Even Twyla Tharp asked for some writers to design the backdrop for her production of "Deuce Coup." Of course this heightened appreciation for graffiti could not last long. Many of the more popular writing groups began to fall apart under the pressure and attention. The camaraderie and collaboration of the writing groups crumbled because of the individual attention many graffiti writers received. Plus, other writers were not pleased with the way in which graffiti was moving into the mainstream. Around 1976, graffiti went back underground.

In 2006 graffiti is rising in popularity again, riding the coattails of the almost obsessive fascination with rap music. While police and youth organizations still fight graffiti on the streets, pieces of it from the 1970s are going on the auction block at Sothebys. Recently a piece by Snake 1 was estimated to sell at $100,000 (Baron, 2000). There are magazines and Web sites dedicated to graffiti. Graffiti adorns CD liner notes, storefront signs, and clothing. It is an integral part of the current hip-hop revolution. At the time of the research, Miguel was in the middle of all of it. He was a writer who appreciated the artistry and longed for the community of the old school of the late 1960s and early 1970s. He was also a writer in tune to the criticisms of graffiti by those in power and influenced by the criminalization of the art form. Finally, he was a writer who saw very few spaces where his writing was accepted or appreciated.

BECOMING A GRAFFITI ARTIST

Miguel developed an interest in graffiti as a creative practice through a community of practice made up of friends and local, national, and international graffiti heroes. Various friends helped him interpret the styles and skills of graffiti as a way of making meaning. In our first interview, Miguel told me the story of how this community of practice influenced his interest in graffiti:

> One night, we was in front of the [elementary school], drinking, you know, smoking weed, whatever. My boy had a can of spray paint. Les. The one who introduce me to graffiti. I seen him tag his name. He used to piece a lot and I said I want to learn...but I wasn't really into it...I was 8 years old, I think. I was like, "Yo. Let me see the can." I tried my name and I couldn't write it, and he was showing me how to write it. So I started every day. I used to go to his house and he used to show me some stuff, and then I think I wrote my name in 14 different places. One of them for a start was the best one I ever did. And then I started hanging with a bunch of people that was doing it. And he was introducing me to a lot of people that was doing graffiti, and they was showing me how to do pieces, backgrounds, and murals. And there was this one guy

who used to live next to me who was teaching me how to airbrush. So I got the hang of that. Then I was like, "I can draw. Why can't I do this?" So one night I'm chilling in my room, listening to the radio until around 2 in the morning, and I was like, "Damn." I started thinking and thinking…I started just making a lot of lines and stuff. I was like, "Damn. That's phat. I've got to try that on a wall." So I got the paint and everything and started painting the wall. Did my name. Came out messed up. I had to repaint over it because I'm still not that good with spray cans…My boy, he came and he was doing his name and he said, "Here, try this nozzle." It was a really skinny nozzle. That day I did my name. It came out nice. And then for the background—I was using "Kash," and I wanted it to fade my name into the background—so he gave me this nozzle. It sprays like fat, really fat, a whole bunch of paint at one time so it's like faded. He showed me how to fade it so I faded it in and stuff. And it started coming out phat. Started doing my characters inside. And I got my rep for the first time doing that. And then it's like "I like this. It expresses the way that I feel." So I kept on doing it and practicing and doing it.

Graffiti and the artists who produce it have always surrounded Miguel. He had close friends who "pieced." His next-door neighbor drew as well and that connection certainly influenced Miguel's decision to pursue the art form. The geographic area in which Miguel lived featured many different kinds of graffiti. His friends and acquaintances introduced him to other communities of practice actively engaged in the art form. Through this network of practitioners, Miguel developed a working knowledge of the craft. It was actually through this interaction with other artists that Miguel began seeing himself as a practitioner: "I can draw. Why can't I do this?" These communities of practice provided space and time for Miguel to experiment with processes of working in the art form. Working with other practitioners pushed him to get his ideas down on paper. Through experimenting with graffiti—"just making a lot of lines and stuff"—Miguel developed a nascent critical perspective on the content of his graffiti writing. The work became a part of him: "It expresses the way that I feel." Finally, this combination of a community of practice, constant experimentation in the form, evaluative feedback from peers, and self-reflection convinced Miguel that he was ready to "perform" his work by creating a public "piece."

However, even at this performance stage, when Miguel determined that he had "to try that on a wall," his work was not polished. Like Ian's performance of "Paranoid Jewish Verse," the act of getting his work up on the wall enabled Miguel to see other techniques and tricks that were important when it came to producing a powerful piece. Here, Miguel's community of practice played a critical role as well. Instead of Miguel having to struggle through honing these skills on his own, he had friends who helped him negotiate the new challenges within his craft by guiding him through particular skills, like fading, and by providing crucial materials for Miguel to be able to do what he wanted to do. In this case, Miguel's friend gave Miguel the nozzles he needed to create the appropriate effect.

This community of practice contributed to Miguel's production of a piece of graffiti of which he was proud. It was also the first piece that got him "rep." Miguel usurped a space—a public wall—not intended for his graffiti. This necessary tension between public and private purposes in order to create is similar to the way Ian usurped class time or Model United Nations time to do his writing. Miguel's community of practice served as an audience that evaluated the content of this work. There was also the larger audience of other graffiti writers within North Philadelphia who saw Miguel's work and liked it.

For several years after this initial foray into the art form, Miguel practiced graffiti in this way. Communities of practice, in the form of "squads," provided space, time, and evaluation for him to deepen his craft. One day while sitting down in his basement, looking at his work, he described some of these squads to me:

> I used to have FDE...FDE meant Fuck Dick Eaters, but they have backstabbed so I had challenged the group and they had to break up. And ABW is a little squad that I started, and I have at least 25 people in there so far. They are doing graffiti and it means America's Baddest Writers. And I'm like in the middle because when...I tag up, I put ABW. When I do pieces, I don't put that because my pieces ain't nothing compared to what my people are, right, my squad. My pieces has nothing to do with the squad. It has to do with me. But when I tag up or when I do a throw-up, or something, I put my squad's name on it, but other than that, I usually just have if I threw it like this right now, I wouldn't just put ABW or representin' Kings or nothing. You can tell really the Kings, when it is the Latin Kings they put an LK or a crown over they name. And a little small one they put by whoever representin' LK that means Latin Kings or KMD.

Squads are similar to the graffiti-writing groups of the mid-1970s. They form in order to support one another's work. However, as Miguel alluded to that day, the writers within these squads do not solely practice within groups. Miguel's individual identity, his style, as a writer was important. In fact, Miguel only recognized his different squads when he either tagged his name or did a quick "throw-up." Miguel reserved his pieces for his name and his name alone because they "[had] to do with me." Consequently, there was a delicate balance between the recognition of his community of practice and his individual production of graffiti. Miguel's pieces were manifestations of his self while his tags and throw-ups served as acknowledgments of his affiliation with particular writing groups.

Toward the end of his description of some of his squads, Miguel connected them with larger, nationally recognized squads like the Almighty Latin King Nation. However, the Almighty Latin King Nation is not simply a squad. They are, in fact, one of the largest gangs in America. Here, Miguel walks a fine line between gang graffiti and graffiti as art, choosing to emphasize the way in which the content of the Almighty Latin King Nation's graffiti influenced his own work. Within this connection, Miguel compared the style choices his squads made to the Almighty Latin King Nation's style. In a way, he used this comparison to both legitimate his own squads' work and at the same time to distinguish his squads' writing from a powerful gang. As I will show, Miguel's interpretation of graffiti's tenuous position in terms of crime and "legitimate" art contributed to his decision to slowly move away from practicing graffiti.

"WE AIN'T THE ONLY ONES THAT THINK THE WAY THAT WE THINK": INTERPRETATION AND GRAFFITI HEROES IN MIGUEL'S PRACTICE

While the community of practice Miguel talked about created space and time for him to practice and perform his graffiti, another crucial community of practice was the graffiti heroes who Miguel either read about, heard about through stories, or met. These social relations played key roles in the development of Miguel's creative practice.

I remember sitting down in Miguel's basement one hot afternoon in September. The door to the backyard was open, and the fan over the glass-top table we sat at was on. Tiny beads of sweat congregated along Miguel's short-cropped hairline. The intensity with which he smoked his Newport Menthols made the room even hotter. The plan that day was for Miguel to take me through some sketches of his pieces and talk with me about the process of designing them. I started the conversation by asking him about a book I gave him the week before—*Getting Up* by Craig Castleman (1982). I considered this book to be one of the best discussions of New York subway graffiti and wanted to get Miguel's opinion on it. I often shared writing on graffiti with Miguel, and Miguel asked me on several occasions to either copy articles or bring copies of my fieldnotes so that he could have them. Miguel understood the history of graffiti. His brother had stolen a book of New York subway graffiti out of a library, and Miguel looked through it regularly to the point where the binding was falling apart. Miguel also read magazines about graffiti. Through this interaction with texts and the conversations he had with friends and his brother, Miguel understood that graffiti came out of the youth gangs in the late 1960s and early 1970s but that the purpose of graffiti shifted during the 1970s. He knew the names and work of the "icons" of the art form; he heard and recounted the stories of how they did their work. He was also very conscious of the way he felt the general public associated graffiti with gangs even today.

I asked Miguel if he had read any of *Getting Up*. Miguel said that he had skimmed some of it. I asked him if anything "caught his eye":

Miguel: The stuff about Lee.
Leif: About Lee? Had you heard about Lee before?
Miguel: Yeah.
Leif: Why or how?
Miguel: Through all of the people that know about graffiti.
Leif: They all talk about Lee?
Miguel: Yeah.
Leif: Really? Why is Lee such a big deal?
Miguel: He got a lot of rep.
Leif: He does?
Miguel: Everybody look up to him. Him and some other boy. I forget his name. He's from New York.
Leif: Lee is from New York, right?
Miguel: Hmm hmmm.
Leif: Why does he have a lot of rep?
Miguel: Because what he does is art. It's not stupid stuff. Like the one he did about his mom. That's rep, man. That's nice. That's art right there.

The "boy" that Miguel couldn't remember is Taki and the piece Miguel referred to is a large "color-blended burner," which Lee dedicated to his mom for her birthday. The piece is of the word "Mom" in bubble letters done to look three-dimensional and glossy. Above the word "Mom," Lee tagged "From Lee too mom." The use of the adverb "too," surprising and syntactically questionable, gives the impression that this amazing work of art is only one of many that he dedicated to his mother.

Lee's style influenced Miguel's graffiti. Through hearing about Lee from other graffiti writers and seeing some of his work in graffiti books and magazines, Miguel included Lee within an imagined community of practice. As Anderson (1983) notes, social relations or communities are not simply constructed out of literal face-to-face interactions. People fashion relationships in their heads as well. In this case, Miguel imagined Lee, Taki, and many other graffiti writers as being part of an extended community that he drew from in order to inform his creative practice.

The way in which Lee unabashedly expressed his love for his mother influenced how Miguel envisioned himself as a graffiti writer. For example, Miguel designed a piece for his nephew that depicted a stack of blocks that spelled his nephew's name with a teddy bear leaning against them. Miguel also envisioned getting a tattoo on his back of two hands placed together in prayer and, surrounding the hands, the names of all of his family members living and dead that he loved. Through his inclusion of Lee and Taki within his communities of practice, Miguel interpreted graffiti and art more broadly to be an expression of love, commitment, and dedication. Lee's work, according to Miguel, exceeded other graffiti writing because it was art as opposed to vandalism. Art in this case incorporated images of family and love, rather than individuality and disrespect. Miguel saw others giving Lee respect for his graffiti because it was art. Because of Miguel's negative history with particular audiences and his graffiti, as I will discuss below, he saw making the move to "elevate" his graffiti to art like Lee's as a way to continue practicing his craft.

That day, Miguel told me the story of getting arrested for his graffiti. I asked him what he would have said to the judge if he had been given the opportunity to plead his own case. In his imagined plea, Miguel makes the argument for considering his graffiti to be art as opposed to vandalism:

> I would be like just because what I do has names, you know, differ-ent pictures in the background and you can't hardly understand what it says because it has lines running through and different colors doesn't mean it's vandalism because I'm expressing the way that I feel. Just like if the guy on TV does the same thing. It's art to y'all and it's art to me, but my stuff ain't art because it has my name and everyone thinks it's from gangs and stuff and posses, symbols from posses, and it's not. It's just me by myself. I'm a one-man army. I'm a soldier by myself. I do what I got to do. I express the way that I feel. To me, I think that it is art. And everybody else

thinks it's vandalism but there are people out there who believe that it is art. And it is people who do art and look at this [his picture] and say that this is art too, professional. But them polices and people who don't know, they think it's vandalism....And they want to press charges saying that this isn't art it's vandalism when it is art. Art is art....Can't press charges for art.

Miguel had a difficult time understanding how his graffiti could be vandalism if its content expressed who he was and how he felt—a particularly American notion coming out of a fervent protection of the freedom of speech. In order to plead his case, Miguel called on an unusual member of his community of practice. He connected his work to the work of Bob Ross, a popular watercolor artist who teaches "how to paint" on public television. The only distinction Miguel saw between Ross's work and his own was the stylistic choice he made to include his name. However, I could see other distinctions as well: for example, the space Miguel appropriated to do his work. As Miguel argued his imaginary case in front of the judge, I wondered if he was making a conscious decision not to include this distinction because he knew that it would jeopardize his argument. Miguel was also conscious of and frustrated by the misinterpretation of his graffiti by "the polices and people who don't know." According to Miguel, this audience connected the content of his work to communities of practice in the form of posses and gangs when in reality, according to Miguel, he worked alone. Actually, Miguel described his graffiti as a battle against these forces that did not understand his art: "I'm a one-man army. I'm a soldier by myself." By connecting him with gangs and posses, the criminal element, it cheapened his work, according to Miguel, and also made it difficult for people to fully understand his graffiti or even consider it to be art.

Finally, Miguel seemed to feel that if these audiences considered his work to be art, then his graffiti would be safe from the law: "Can't press charges for art." This phrase simplifies a rather complicated situation because underneath it all, Miguel was not looking for full acceptance of his writing. Miguel recognized the importance of graffiti being transgressive in terms of the space it occupied. Here, Miguel made a case in a particular space, an imaginary courtroom, for a particular audience: a judge. Miguel knows how to talk about the content of his work within the language of "legitimate" art. In a way, he's a good lawyer. However, as I will show, Miguel's recognition of the complexity of his situation pushes him to search out new spaces that are not as transgressive in order to engage in his creative practice, thus changing the style and ultimately the practice itself over time.

Confusion and Clarity: The Importance of
Experimentation and Performance

While the heroes of old school graffiti influenced Miguel and helped shape his understanding of the distinction between vandalism and art, he also appreciated and was drawn to the "new school" contemporary style of graffiti, often termed *Confusion*. Relationships with other artists introduced Miguel to this particular style of graffiti. This community of practice also influenced how Miguel experimented with graffiti and opened up possible new spaces for practicing and performing his work.

Confusion is an appropriate name for this style, particularly from the perspective of those outside of the intended audience, because part of the goal of writing in *Confusion* is to deceive the viewer visually. Conquergood writes,

> Graffiti writing is a very ambivalent form of visual communication that pivots on a dialectic between display and disguise, visibility and veiling, spectacle and secrecy; it is communication that is simultaneously conspicuous and camouflaged…youth go to great lengths and risk to make spectacles out of their writing on the wall even as they take care to mask their messages. (1997, p. 355)

In old school graffiti, writers kept their real identities hidden by using writing names usually with a street number connected to it: Lee 158, for example. In *Confusion*, the writer embeds his or her name in a series of carefully drawn lines. Some lines have arrows pointing in different directions. Some of these lines contribute to forming the letter of the name. Others purposefully lead you away from deciphering the letters. Paradoxically, like most graffiti, pieces done in *Confusion* have a large and varied audience because it is public in nature but at the same time only a limited number of that audience can actually read the literal message of the piece.

From this new school of graffiti practitioners, Miguel respected a local graffiti artist named DanOne. Unlike the bubble letters and cartoon characters of old school graffiti, DanOne's work is geometric and angular in design. A form of the number 1 that rises up in the middle of the work characterizes most of his pieces. One can see many of DanOne's pieces occupying space on 5th Street in North Philadelphia, the main thoroughfare through Little Puerto Rico. For much of this work, DanOne gets permission from whomever "owns" the wall in order for him to do a piece. DanOne has also crossed over to displaying his work on canvas. Miguel and I had a chance to see some of DanOne's work on canvas, as well as two other local graffiti artists', at an alternative art gallery in downtown Philadelphia.

In this opening, the pieces were carefully hung on the walls around the café of the performance space. Softly illuminated from above and placed far enough apart so that each work had its own space, the graffiti assumed an entirely different purpose in my eyes. Graffiti had become "museumified" and through that process exuded a different aura of professionalism and authority from the way in which graffiti is appreciated on the street by outside observers. Even the medium used, the glossy oil-based paint, changed the feeling of the graffiti for me.

Miguel walked around this space, stopping at each piece and scrutinizing it, putting his face sometimes within inches of the painting, following the lines with his eyes. There were at least 15 other people in the gallery, looking at the work. It was incredibly quiet, reverential in a way. Every now and then Miguel would whisper to me, "That's phat!" He was particularly drawn to one piece where the name was painted like shattered glass. Later, while thumbing through the guest "blackbook" of the exhibit, Miguel told me that he had met DanOne once at Casa, the youth center Miguel went to. Miguel said that DanOne had given him "props" for a shirt Miguel had airbrushed.

Several days later, while hanging out at Miguel's house, he told me he asked his step-pop to buy some stretched canvas for him. The experience of seeing DanOne's graffiti on canvas started Miguel thinking about what would happen if he put his graffiti on canvas. Having the image on the medium of canvas and carefully hung on a wall, in Miguel's mind, gave it a legitimacy that his work on the walls of his school, for example, did not. Through this form of appreciation, graffiti was able to exist within public spaces. He witnessed people taking time to study graffiti on canvas, and he wanted his work to demand that kind of respect. Curiously, Miguel's understanding of legitimating/purifying his graffiti by changing the medium on which it was drawn was limited to the act of drawing on canvas. He had not planned, nor did he know exactly how to go about or have the support network needed, to display his work anywhere. Without communities of practice to support this shift, an audience to look at and evaluate his work, or a space to "hang" his graffiti, I wondered how long he would be able to continue the work.

As I mentioned briefly above, communities of practice do not necessarily involve face-to-face interaction between people. Miguel associated himself with people who share his interest in graffiti specifically and art more generally, similarly to the way Anderson (1983) argues that people identify with a particular "political community." While Miguel may never meet many of the practitioners who make up his "imagined" social network (Taki, Lee, and the other graffiti artists in the gallery show, for example), he did interact with them through reading, evoking them in conversation, reflecting on their work, and allowing their style to inform his own. Specifically, Miguel "conferred" with Taki and Lee, interpreting their work to legitimate his own graffiti.

Reflecting on and interpreting the way in which the juvenile justice system forced a negative connotation on his creative practice encouraged Miguel to shift his graffiti from walls to canvas. Miguel was conscious of the way in which the court connected him to gangs and posses through his work. He saw canvas as a performance space that had the potential of disassociating himself from the negative connotations of graffiti and gangs.

INSTITUTIONAL INFLUENCE: INTERPRETING GRAFFITI AS ART

Many spaces of activity influenced Miguel's move to interpret graffiti as art. In fact, it is the interplay between contested and supportive spaces, and the communities of practice within these spaces, that convinced Miguel of the need to transform his graffiti into legitimate "art." Finally, the lack of space for Miguel to practice graffiti contributed to this transformation as well.

Casa

Before Miguel and I started our research project, Miguel "did his time" for a vandalism charge in a youth center, Casa, located not too far from Miguel's house. This youth center specialized in working with "at-risk" Puerto Rican youth. In his time at Casa, Miguel came to know and eventually respect one of the teachers he worked with. Realizing that most of the youth in her class were involved in graffiti, the teacher designed a class on its history. The teacher and students explored the connection between petroglyphs and modern graffiti content. At Casa, Miguel learned that graffiti was not simply an illegal act, but that it was an art form with a long and complex history. In this case, Casa appropriated the term "art" and connected it with graffiti in order to "raise" it to a level of culture that many within mainstream society do not. Another way in which the teacher legitimated graffiti was through an assignment in which the students were to represent their graffiti style on paper and write about why they liked graffiti.

In this assignment, Miguel chose to include a sketch of a piece for his graffiti name "Kash." He also drew a lizardlike creature holding what appeared to be either a can of spray paint or a 40-ounce bottle of beer. Over the sketch of his name was a photograph of Miguel standing outside of the high school where the Casa class took place. Miguel was standing at about a 45-degree angle to the camera. He wore his standard t-shirt, baggy blue jeans, and Timberland boots. His hands were in his pockets. There was no smile on his face—his mouth was a straight line. He squinted at the camera, not because the sun was in his eyes, though it was a sunny day, but because that was the way he looked at you. It was a serious, hard look.

To the left of the picture was Miguel's reason for liking graffiti. It was handwritten by Miguel in careful, blocked print and was distinctly different from the quick script of his tags: "I like graffiti because it is like art and I can show the way I feel." Above his photograph, Miguel wrote his name the way a graffiti writer might do next to one of his pieces—fat print letters with an arrow that led to the squad he was affiliated to: "M.O.B!" Interestingly he also wrote his name next to the sketch of the piece below the photograph and next to his real name, Miguel, he also wrote "Kash" with an arrow leading to "ABW!!" Within this assignment, Miguel represented multiple sources that informed his practice. Miguel incorporated Casa's point that graffiti was an important and legitimate way to express one's feelings. Miguel also included the numerous communities of practice connected to his work. The piece was an interesting blending of institutional and communal people and spaces that supported his work.

The Juvenile Justice System and School

Miguel's interpretation of his interactions with the juvenile justice system certainly influenced the way he experimented with the form and his ultimate decision to move away from graffiti altogether. During a year when art galleries featured local graffiti artists, and national magazines like *Newsweek* printed articles about the money graffiti artists made for their work, the police arrested Miguel for his graffiti. I asked Miguel to tell me the story behind the arrest:

> The cops like, "You come down," and I was like, "Not until I'm done. I'm going to finish this piece."...Then I went down and I had a whole thing of nozzles and I didn't want to get locked up so I threw them into my boy's window and they let me go through my house down...They grabbed the nozzles and all the spray cans and everything....[A] teacher at [our] school was like, "The name was on my wall and it wasn't there before." And I was like, "Damn. Did you put my name on the school?"

And [my friend] was like, "Yeah." So I was like, "See? Now I'm going to get busted for that too." Then [the police] started pinning my names to everything…They told me I was going to do 24 months and then when I went to court, they told me I was going to do 3 years. They dropped it down to 6 months' probation at the halfway house, Casa.

Miguel also told me what happened at the police station:

When we got locked up…the police was like, "You ever been locked up before?" I was like, "Nah." "You know what your fingerprints are from? A stolen car." I said, "Yo, I haven't stolen no cars." Well, they were like, "We got your hand on a stolen car that's how we got your fingerprints." I was like, "What you mean? I don't steal no cars." He was like, "Yo, you ain't coming out any time soon." I was like, "Yo, I didn't steal no car. You better get proof. You better get somebody saying I stole the car because I didn't do shit. You can't lock me up for not stealing shit." So when they took me to the guys that investigate graffiti and vandalism and stolen cars and stuff, my boy, his record, because he got locked up four times before I did, it was from stolen cars. He had stole 32 cars. Of course, they had his fingerprints and what screwed me was because the same car they had got the fingerprints from, his fingerprints were on it too so they tried to put that on me. I was like, "Yo, I didn't steal no car."…They pulled out the blackbook and started showing me pictures and stuff of all of the places I did graffiti. I said, "I don't remember I did that there." I didn't even remember it. Then they showed me a picture in the blackbook of all the places my boy did and I was like, "Damn, my name was next to his a lot of times." Then they showed me all of the cars he had stolen and that was like a book like that [holding out his fingers about an inch apart to show thickness]. And I was like, "Oh man, I ain't getting out no time soon." Then they showed me the car that had my fingerprints. It was a '95 Saturn…I said, "Yo, I never seen that car before." So I said, "I could have been leaning on it that's why." They said, "But your hands were on the steering wheel." What the hell was I supposed to say? So I stayed quiet. They was like, "We ain't going to press charges on you because we ain't got no proof that you were the one that stole it" because they caught my boy in that car. So they dropped the charge…So I was cool. And then they were calling the study center to see if they wanted to place me there for 24 months.

Miguel reflected on the police's treatment and the way they framed his work. He thought about their use of language to determine what were and what were not appropriate forms of expression. This confrontation with the law made Miguel change his strategy in terms of the content of his graffiti. While on the surface he often talked about how he didn't "give a fuck" about what anybody thought—"If they don't like it they can go play with themselves in the corner. I don't care. To me, it's art. If nobody like it, I am my own audience. I like what I do. I think of it as art"—he was sensitive to how the police and the court negatively evaluated his work. Their reaction made him look differently at the content of the graffiti that he saw every day at school. Writing his name in *Confusion*, with its images of dragons and demons and the use of profanity within the pieces and tags, the court and police interpreted all of this as vandalism. Miguel did not want his graffiti to be interpreted as vandalism. So he made a conscious effort to experiment with a different kind of graffiti:

Miguel: Everything I am going to do is not going to be my name or nothing. It's going to be pictures and stuff. I want to do it on canvas like we saw…I haven't got my money to buy my stuff yet. I plan on doing that pretty soon. And do different stuff, not just my name. Not just dragons on the back of demons. For little kids and stuff, like teddy bears and stuff. My little nephew's name. I was hooking that up before I got locked up. I mean, it was looking nice, but I got mad because they kept painting over the same wall that I kept doing every day. They kept painting over it, and I didn't like that because it was my nephew's name. It wasn't nobody's property. It was just the people in the neighborhood didn't like it. So they started painting over it and I was ticked off. I started finding out who was doing it and I started writing on their house.

Leif: Why did you do that?

Miguel: Because I was mad. Because it's nobody's property, man. It was art because I had drew teddy bears and stuff, make it look nice with blocks. Every block had a letter of his name in it and stuff. I did it four times in the same…it was just a regular wall. It wasn't even no home or nothing to it. It was just a wall there. They kept painting over it, man. Eventually they knocked down the wall. My nephew's name ain't there no more.

Miguel also interpreted from his confrontation with the police that one of the things that got him caught was the use of his name in his work. Unlike most graffiti artists who choose one name and stick with it for a long period of time, Miguel constantly experimented with many different names: Kash, Omas, Sin, Flash, and eventually Reaper. Miguel said to me at one point that he had over 40 names that he had created for himself. The variety of names and the shifting of characters fit the life that Miguel lived at the time of the research. Not only did he dream up all kinds of different names for himself, but he also dreamed about the different places he could live, the different kinds of jobs that he wanted, the future. Miguel's life at the time of this research was in a constant state of flux that contributed to the ambiguity inherent in much of what he chose to do. In addition, the lack of a consistent and safe space to engage in the creative practice of graffiti certainly contributed to his desire to experiment with different names as well as different creative practices.

Miguel began to evaluate the content of other graffiti writers and identify his own work in opposition to other graffiti and graffiti writers. During one of our many one-on-one basketball games, Miguel explained his frustration to me:

Miguel: I like doing it [referring to his graffiti], but people mess up everything for everybody.

Leif: Tell me about why you have made that decision [to stop doing graffiti].

Miguel: Let me put it like this. See that's art right there [pointing to one of his pieces]. This ain't [pointing at one of his tags]. At school, they be putting stupid shit like "suck my dick," "bitch ass niggers," and whatnot, and right there that's vandalism. So when I do something like this [pointing to his piece], they are going to think it's vandalism. I can't show people it's not vandalism if people are doing stupid shit like that. So it's not worth it. I see the people painting the bathroom walls like every day. Every day they have stupid shit on it. Stupid like that [pointing at his tag]. It's not worth it. So I was like, "You know what, man, I am going to stop doing graffiti." These niggers, they mess it up for everybody.

Leif: What do you think about the other graffiti artists who are doing stuff like this [pointing to Miguel's piece]? Why are they still doing it?

Miguel: Everybody have different opinions for different things. They do shit like that [pointing to the tag], it's not worth me doing something like this [pointing to his piece]. They are going to go over it with that [referring to the tag]. I don't like that. That's why I haven't started doing stuff like this again. It's not worth it. Niggers always got to mess it up.

By this time, the court's interpretation of what constituted vandalism and art as well as Miguel's growing discomfort with other forms of graffiti had permeated Miguel's interpretation of the art form. In part, he reflected on his work and the work of other graffiti artists through the evaluative lens of the court. Miguel also sensed that no matter how artful his work was, no matter how he changed the content or style of it, it would be considered vandalism. The taggers who Miguel felt would inevitably write over his pieces pushed him out or usurped his work space.

Miguel also witnessed the destructive quality of what people on the outside of the practice termed vandalism. Miguel did not associate himself with the bathroom taggers who made the maintenance people paint the school bathrooms every day. He labeled their vandalism graffiti. Miguel also indicated that he got the sense that the school administration and the juvenile justice system lumped him in with this group, ascribing an association with a community of practice of which Miguel did not want to be a part. Miguel felt that there were few if any spaces for him to practice his graffiti. While his "boys" may have appreciated the content of his work, the audience that "policed" the space—the school administration, NTAs (nonteaching assistants), teachers, and maintenance people—was not able to distinguish between the vandalism that Miguel described and his art.

As I have discussed, there were important spaces connected to his graffiti writing that put Miguel in contact with various communities of practice as well as encouraged him to reflect on and evaluate his life and his work. Casa provided a space for Miguel to see the lineage of his writing, which legitimated it through connecting the content of the practice to an extended history quite removed from "the streets." Within the space of Casa, Miguel also worked with other graffiti writers, thus extending his already growing community of practice. With this kind of support, one would think that Miguel had the foundation necessary to continue refining his practice. However, the imposing space of the courtroom, as well as jail, complicated Miguel's interest in graffiti. Through their categorization of Miguel's work as well as their continued surveillance of him, Miguel developed a heightened critical take on the content of his own graffiti and the graffiti writing of others. In addition, Miguel's experience with the juvenile justice system made him realize the power and at the same time the liability that his name embodied in connection to his creative practice. Finally, other graffiti writers, a community of practice one assumes would play a supportive role, restricted Miguel's practice space by writing over his work. This refutation of the content of his practice played a role in Miguel experimenting with new forms of creative practice, one of them being tattooing his skin.

MIGUEL'S MOVE FROM GRAFFITI TO TATTOOING

In fear of getting arrested again, Miguel literally locked himself in his house for several months and did not go to school or hang out with his friends. The only time he left the house was to run errands for his mother, spend the day with his step-pop at his job as a maintenance man at a local motel, or visit his sister. Without the resources of a community of practice, Miguel's graffiti writing did not have the lifeblood needed to sustain itself. As a result, Miguel experimented with a variety of diffuse projects. He started drawing pictures for his family. He showed me a long, rectangular piece of white presentation board. On it was an homage to his brothers. He also showed me several pieces of 8½-by-11 inch sheets of white paper on which he had drawn different Disney characters for his nieces and nephews. Much of this work he did while visiting his sister, Miguel told me. He also developed an interest in tattooing.

In what follows, I describe Miguel's home life to link the complex relationship between space and Miguel's experimenting with model building, fly tying, airbrushing, and, ultimately, tattooing. Miguel's house, in particular his room, was a space embedded in a larger domestic world. In this world, Miguel's mother and other family members required him to share space. Often, they made Miguel share space for extended periods of time. This tension between the need to share a space and Miguel's desire to have a space that he controlled challenged Miguel's ability to develop a sustainable practice for producing graffiti on canvas that, in turn, made it difficult for Miguel to engage in this form of creative practice. Instead, Miguel employed tactics and strategies to experiment with discreet projects that used time and space in ways that co-exist with the other important demands of his life. Miguel moved his creative practice to these discreet projects as a way of ordering his life at a time when Miguel felt a sense of chaos and lack of control in relation to his wants and needs and the demands of his family.

The Significance of Home

Miguel's family lived in a small row house along a street across from a park in which Miguel played basketball and sometimes hung out with his friends. When you walked into Miguel's house, you walked into the living room. A coffee table was in the center of the room and an entertainment center was against the far wall. To the right of the living room was the kitchen. A small kitchen table occupied the space between the far wall and the outside wall. Two could sit comfortably there. Often, Miguel's mom used the table to rest the large buckets of rice she had in order to be able to scoop it out for the meal that night. The kitchen was cramped, and almost every time I visited, there was something aromatic cooking: turkey, beans, rice, pork chops sizzling in a frying pan. The stairs leading to the basement were off of the kitchen.

If one were to walk directly through the living room, one would walk into Miguel's room. A large four-poster bed took up most of it. A dresser lined the wall along with a TV with a PlayStation. A small poster of Michael Jordan was on the wall along with a picture of Miguel on a baseball team. There was a piece of graffiti that Miguel drew on the wall as well: a piece by "Kash." Miguel first drew the name in red and black and then cut it out, placing it on a paper background to give it a three-dimensional look. This piece hung over Miguel's bed. On his dresser were several model cars in different stages of construction. On his dresser were several different kinds of cologne. I asked him why he had so many different kinds:

Miguel: It makes me smell good.

Leif: What's your favorite kind?

Miguel: Tommy and…[points to another bottle I can't see]

Leif: Tommy and that [referring to the bottle that I can't see]? Why?

Miguel: 'Cause it's the shit. Tommy's all right, but you can't beat Navy. Navy will beat its ass.

Leif: Do you wear it for certain things?

Miguel: One for playing ball. Another one for getting dressed up to go out.

Leif: What do you wear to go out?

Miguel: I use Cuba, Navy, some special cologne that my brother got. I use all kinds of shit. I use to have [indecipherable], man, that was a good ass cologne, yo, for when you run ball. The more you sweat the more you smell good.

Leif: I was going to ask you. I had never thought about putting on cologne when I play basketball.

Miguel: You don't want to stink, man, especially if you meet a girl. When I get through playing basketball, too, I always take a shower.

Cintron discusses neatness and cleanliness in relation to the Mexican-American youth in his study. He argues that the youth keep their cars fanatically clean as a way of "express[ing] control, dominance over nature and its plenitude of decay" (Cintron, 1997, p. 118). On one level, Miguel wore cologne in order to appear attractive to "girls." I also see a connection between his style of graffiti and his move to canvas with the need he felt to "smell good." Perhaps these moves were how Miguel created order in a time of disorder as well as how he recognized the significance of appearances. Miguel occupied space through smell and in this way he exuded an ordered and controlled self. Cintron suggests that the fastidious attention to the neat and clean in terms of the youth in his study is a desire to cover up "all those traces of raggedness and decay that lurked in private spaces" (p. 118). Miguel employed a similar tactic here. In this case, the untidiness of the graffiti he saw at school, his home life, and his experience with the juvenile justice system all contributed to Miguel's move to make things neat and clean, not only through the use of cologne but also through his shift to canvas, then into discreet creative projects in the form of model building, fly tying, and painting his boots, and eventually to tattooing his skin.

On this particular day, clothes were strewn about Miguel's room. Miguel said he did not like keeping his room this way. His uncle was visiting. They did not get to sleep until around 4 in the morning, and Miguel said that his uncle messed the room up.

While Miguel spent hours and a considerable amount of money to decorate his space, other members of the family would either share the space with him or force him to move out for an unspecified amount of time. Our last "official" meeting was perhaps the most telling regarding how this constant shuffling around and lack of personal space in the home affected Miguel.

I got to the door and could see Miguel laid out, in the middle of the living room, on the blue blow-up mattress that he slept on when other people stayed in his room. If anyone in the house wanted to get anywhere, they had to essentially walk over Miguel. When I knocked on the door, Miguel slowly pulled himself up off the mattress, rubbed his eyes, and opened the door and told me to come in. We had planned for Miguel to take me on a tour of his room. I asked Miguel if he could take me on that tour and he said that he could not because the baby was sleeping in there. Miguel told me that the baby belonged to his cousin Louis. Louis was incarcerated for a five-year sentence, and Miguel's aunt came back down from Connecticut to take care of the baby while Louis served his time. Miguel said that he had not been sleeping in his room for four months, and he was frustrated about it—so frustrated that he told his mom the night before that if he did not get his room back, he was going to move out.

Miguel suggested we go down to the basement and talk because his room was occupied. Kitchen cabinets and various tools from the current kitchen-remodeling job rested on the large table in the basement as well as on the floor. When Miguel got down there and saw the clutter he said, "I hate this shit." We went back upstairs and walked out to the basketball courts to talk.

Leif:	How do you feel about not being able to be in your room for four months?
Miguel:	I'm frustrated right now, yo.
Leif:	I can understand that. You've been spending a lot of time on that room, putting stuff up…
Miguel:	And I don't even get to enjoy that shit.
Leif:	Yeah.
Miguel:	I'm about to move out. I told my mom, "Look, I am going to give you a certain amount of time to get my room back or I'm leaving." I told her like that last night.
Leif:	Yeah?
Miguel:	She said, "All right, all right." I said, "I'm not playing, yo." I love them and all, man, but we've got a sofa bed downstairs. You go sleep downstairs. It's my fucking room. I can't sleep in my boxers, yo. Especially when it starts to get hot. I can't be relaxed. I can't do that, man.
Leif:	Because you're sleeping out in the middle…
Miguel:	Yo, I am getting mad.
Leif:	What if you said no, they just can't sleep in your room? Is that possible?
Miguel:	I would, but then my mom would hate me for that. She would never forgive me. I told her if I don't get my room back, I am leaving. I'm not playing. I don't give a fuck. I like my fucking room, you know?

The necessity for Miguel to share space precipitated many things. For one, it made it difficult for Miguel to have space and time to experiment with graffiti writing on canvas. Because other people used his room, he could not leave his canvas or assorted supplies out. The other two spaces, the living room and basement, were shared as well. He could not leave his drawing, for example, on the coffee table because other people used that space. The family often used the basement table to hold projects in various states of completion. For example, Miguel's mom would leave the ceramic figurines she was painting on the table to dry. Consequently, it was difficult for Miguel to find space he could use for prolonged periods of time to do creative work. Therefore, the work had to be done in quick bursts of activity—little experiments that could be done and put away.

While Ian could take six months in order to craft a poem, having the privilege of personal space to work, Miguel did not have that luxury. He had to be an opportunist in a different sense. Miguel had to appropriate a different kind of time and space. Once graffiti became problematic for Miguel, he experimented with discreet, small, one-off projects that were easily transportable and small enough to be able to tuck away in drawers or under the bed. A good example of this kind of work were the pictures he would draw and leave at his sister's during his frequent visits there. Another good example were the flies he tied for fishing: each one delicate looking and meticulously done, an exercise in complete control—another possible way of making life neat, clean, and manageable.

The importance of sharing space in Miguel's family required Miguel to experiment differently than Ian who lived a middle-class life. Miguel used the limited personal space and time that he felt he had to do mini-projects. For example, when he was finished tying the flies, they fit in a drawer, tucked away from the curious fingers of nieces and nephews or other family members using his room. He also devoted creative time to redesigning his Timberland boots by airbrushing them. Miguel was the only one who wore these boots so the possibility of others taking them in the middle of the project was slim.

Miguel often stayed up late finishing a model, drafting a piece on canvas or in his sketchbook, or painting his boots. Then there would be long stretches of inactivity related to his creative practice. Instead, Miguel spent his time accompanying family members to the doctor, working with his brothers on remodeling houses, working with his stepbrother on fixing cars, and thinking about all the other things he would rather do. A pattern with all three youth and their creative practices is the necessity to negotiate their creative work around the demands of family life.

Even amid these challenges, the desire to make meaning through writing and drawing did not pass. Cintron writes, "Graffiti is the evidence of an intense need to acquire power and voice" (Cintron, 1997, p. 186). While Miguel tired of fighting the systems of exclusion, he did not stop working. He did not stop creating vehicles for acquiring power and voice. He made the choice to shift his work once more, this time to both an intensely personal and communal space.

FROM DISCREET PROJECTS TO SKIN

By the end of the research, Miguel shifted his creative practice to experimenting with tattooing. He would sketch them and then have his brother or friend draw them on his skin. Miguel's interpretation of the negative reception of his graffiti as well as the difficulty to find space and time to write encouraged him to move to a "canvas" that was his property and could not be evaluated in the same way by the dominant society. Through this shift, Miguel also developed a new community of practice—his friends and family—in the processes of creative production. The practice of tattooing opened up new opportunities for interpretation, performance, reflection, and evaluation. In addition, tattooing is the ultimate act of appropriating space and time. Tattooing freezes space and time for Miguel, making it possible to engage in a creative practice when other space and time that is not directly connected to his body are difficult to come by. Finally, this move to tattooing is striking because it further exposes ways in which class mediates the ways in which interpretation, reflection, evaluation, and performance are employed in a creative practice. In order to show how Miguel's shift from public space to private bodily form employs interpretation, performance, reflection, and evaluation as well as reconfigures the community of practice of his creative practice, I provide a vignette of Miguel's brother, Carlos, giving Miguel a tattoo.

The tattoo was a cross drawn in black ink with the letter "V" and the letter "L" adjacent to one another within the right angles of the cross. Miguel designed the cross himself. He showed me the piece of onionskin that he had drawn it on. Miguel told me that, many times, people who do tattoos will take the sketch, rub some deodorant on the place where the person wants the tattoo, and then lay the sketch over the deodorant. This process leaves an imprint of the sketch on the skin and then the person doing the tattoo has a model from which to work. For this tattoo, Miguel had many different models because most of the men in his family have the same tattoo.

We sat down at the kitchen table in Carlos's house. Nidia, Carlos's sister, offered us coffee, in Carlos's words, "Puerto Rican style—sweet, con leche." She gave Carlos a coffee cup with "Big Boss" written on it. The kitchen table took up most of the space. Carlos told me to sit in the nice chair as I was "dressed the nicest." Miguel sat at the opposite end from me, and Carlos sat between us. Carlos talked with his sister about several things in Spanish. While Carlos got the supplies ready—a piece of sewing thread, a sewing needle, black mechanical tape, a piece of paper towel, and black ink—Miguel's nieces and nephews came in. One of his nephews asked about my tape recorder. I told him that I was doing some research with Miguel, and Carlos joked, "Yeah, he's a private investigator."

Carlos took the needle and waved it under the flame of his cigarette lighter for a few seconds. He then wrapped the white thread around the sharp tip. After making sure that the thread was secure, Carlos put the needle down and wrapped the tip of his left pointer finger with black mechanical tape. He twisted off the top to the black ink, picked the needle back up, dipped it into the ink, turned to Miguel and said, "Ready for the pain, dog?" Miguel smiled and gripped the side of the table with his other hand.

I had never experienced someone getting a tattoo "prison style." It looked incredibly painful. Essentially, the objective is to inject ink underneath the skin, using the needle and thread that Carlos prepared. In order to do that, Carlos had to first soak the needle in the ink and then, with amazing force, jam the needle underneath the skin, pulling upward at the end so that the ink would catch. "It grabs the ink. It absorbs the ink, and when you push it in…it's like, if it was a sponge. You know a sponge absorbs water, and you press on it and the water comes out? It's the same thing with the needle. The thread absorbs it and when you push it in. It goes in there. That's why I keep dipping it," Carlos said.

Carlos would first inject the ink under the skin and then scrape the surface of the skin to help accentuate the line. He seemed to be seasoned at this. I could tell by the way in which he almost blindly assembled the different tools and carried on several conversations at the same time. He informed me that he had done most of his own tattoos in the same way. Carlos did many of his tattoos when he was angry and because he likes to feel pain, he said. He learned in prison, a place he had been on and off since he was a teenager. He was 26 at the time of this event.

I could tell from the way that Miguel looked, and the way he kept on asking Carlos if it looked all right, that this was a new experience for him. Carlos poked the needle into Miguel's hand, jamming it up under the skin and then pulling upward in order for the ink to catch. He dipped the needle back into the ink and jabbed it in again. Miguel checked Carlos's progress after every application. Carlos dipped the needle into the ink again and held Miguel's hand as he jabbed the needle into Miguel's skin, grimacing slightly as he lifted the needle under the skin. Miguel put his head down and looked at me as his brother did it. He said that he could see the needle underneath his skin. "That hurts like a motherfucker," Miguel said. "Feels good, doesn't it," Carlos replied.

During the procedure, Miguel's nieces and nephews came back to the kitchen. Miguel's niece, a tall, thin girl, looked at the tattoo. Her eyes grew wide and she said, "Phat!" Miguel's two nephews looked and grimaced in pain, laughing uncomfortably. The younger nephew told Carlos that he did not want him doing tattoos anymore. Miguel screamed with the next jab, and this nephew said, "Be a man, not a woman." Carlos then looked up from Miguel's hand and asked the nephew if he had done his homework. He said that he did. Carlos asked if he had any spelling words. He said he did not. He had social studies "from that boring teacher" and math. Carlos questioned, "You don't have any spelling words?" His nephew shrugged his shoulders and said that he had the same ones from last week. Then all three scrambled out of the kitchen to go outside and play in the snow.

Once the niece and two nephews had left in a burst of noise and movement, Miguel said, "They are smart as hell, yo!" I nodded. Miguel continued by explaining that they were in the gifted classes in school. "When you ask them spelling words," Miguel said, "you don't even have to give the word. You just have to say the number and they can give you the word, spell it, and give the definition." Miguel smiled. "God bless them," he said.

Every now and then, Miguel screamed out as Carlos pushed the needle under his skin. But at the same time, there was a strange calmness to the event. Carlos spoke softly the whole time, almost under his breath. He focused on Miguel's hand, and only looked up when one of his nieces or nephews came in to ask him a question.

After finishing one of the long lines of the cross, Carlos lifted Miguel's hand to take a look at his work. Miguel said, "How is it?" and pulled his hand toward himself to judge. "It's perfect, man. It's perfect," Carlos said.

Carlos mentioned that he had tried to tell Miguel that he needed to "get his education" and do something with his life. He said that nobody listens to a person who has not done it himself. Carlos said, "Why should anybody trust me if I don't have a high school or college diploma?" "There is no life here," he continued. He did not want his kids growing up here. "Believe me," he said. "If you have seen what I have seen."

It should come as no surprise that Miguel's desire to get a tattoo was in part influenced by Carlos, not only because Carlos had his own tattoos but also because of the way Carlos reflected on his life and the way in which he acted like another father figure for Miguel. At one point, Miguel lived with Carlos when their parents were separating. "He's more of a father to me than my own pop," Miguel said.

While Carlos worked, he interpreted the significance of the cross: "The letters are a family symbol." He looked up from the tattoo, smiled, and asked Nidia to "leave the premises." She looked back at him and asked him to say please. He smiled again and said, "Please." Nidia smirked, "Thank you," wiped her hands off on the tablecloth, and walked into the living room where the nieces and nephews were.

Carlos: Have you ever seen the movie *Blood In, Blood Out*?

Leif: No.

Carlos: Anyway, this symbol is…it's a nationwide symbol. Like a lot of family that is true to your family would have a symbol like this, especially my family. You see, we look out for one another. We'll take anybody's back. Like, we'll give our life…

Miguel: He knows the squad [referring to the group Carlos is referencing]. He gave me the book [referring to the book *Always Running: Gang Days in L.A.*].

Carlos: OK, we'll give our life to whatever. If anything happens to him [pointing to Miguel with the needle], I'll take the blame for it. You know what I mean? Somebody going to try to kill him, I'm going to do it before they try to get him. That's the way we feel. That's the way our whole family feels. And like them letters have been in our family for, like I said, years. And then we saw that they made a movie about it [referring to *Blood In, Blood Out*]. And then in L.A., they got the same symbols.

Leif: Oh, really?

Carlos: Yeah. So now, we feel…I don't know how to explain it…we feel more, how do you say, "safer now" because we know that this shit is spreading everywhere. You know what I mean? Like everybody that has this symbol, that's what it really means. It means that you will be there for the person, your family, you'll do anything. If anything happens, you're there. Whoever punks out? I feel sorry for them.

Miguel: They're catching it.

Carlos: They're catching it. It don't matter if they're family or not.

Miguel: He already know what the "VL" means. He should know. He gave me a book about it [referring again to *Always Running*].

Leif: Is it in *Getting Up*? The book I gave you?

Miguel: *Always Running*.

Leif: Oh, *Always Running*. It's in there? Did you read it?

Miguel: I read some stuff in it.

Leif: What did you think?

Miguel: [smiling] It was good, man.

Leif: They talk about it in *Always Running* [laugh]?

Miguel: VL means…

Carlos: Vatos Locos, man.

Miguel: Vatos Locos.

Carlos: We be some crazy motherfuckers. That's what it means. And we know a lot of people in New York that got this symbol. Connecticut. We found out now, because of the book, we found out that L.A.'s got the symbol. A lot of people got these symbols and don't really....A lot of people don't know what it means until you really talk to the person that got it or that book. That book means a lot. That book made us happy. After we read it and shit, we found out a lot of shit about it. It means we ain't the only ones that think the way that we think. You know what I mean?

There was a pause in the conversation. Miguel told Carlos that it hurt and Carlos said, "You got to relax, man." He jabbed the needle in again and continued:

Carlos: These symbols, you really got to earn these symbols. He didn't earn it, but, since he's family, it's cool. Like I know couple boys in jail that got it. A lot of people get crazy shit on their hands. They just get it because…a lot of people get symbols on their hands because they in a gang. This is like, to us, it's a family thing. We already know what it means. At least, that's our point of view of what it means. That's why we got it. You've seen my uncle. My uncle's got it. My brother got it. I didn't get mine yet. I was supposed to get mine before anybody.

Miguel gasped as he watched Carlos plunge the needle in yet again. Carlos smiled, "Feels good, doesn't it." Miguel responded, "I ain't feeling it, yo. I'm just feeling this tingling feeling running up my hand." Carlos then jabbed it in especially hard. Miguel shouted, "I felt that motherfucker. You really stuck that bitch in!"

By the time Carlos finished, the flesh around Miguel's tattoo was red and swollen. In the middle of this puffy flesh was the black cross, a geometric mix of sharp angles and fluid arcs. As Carlos said, most males in Miguel's family have this tattoo. All of them have the tattoo in the same place: the fleshy part of the right hand, between the thumb and forefinger.

The sources that Carlos and Miguel interpret in order to make this cross meaningful are multiple and diverse. Movies, various books, experiences in prison, and the familial tradition all contribute to their interpretation of what the cross means. Ultimately, Carlos and Miguel assemble these disparate sources to create a sense of safety. The fact that Carlos and Miguel are able to locate their symbol in multiple (con)texts legitimates the thoughts and feelings that they associate with it. At the same time, they make a distinction between the more common gang association and their use of the sign. VL is also the symbol for one of the largest gangs in the nation: the Vice Lords. Is there a connection? Perhaps, though I did not witness Miguel engage in any gang-related activity while working with him for that year and a half. Regardless, the careful distinction that Carlos and Miguel make between their use of the sign and its wider meaning points to the complexity of the practice. To them, the cross symbolizes a particular kind of community of practice. It is a "family thing."

While experimenting with the style of his graffiti, while interpreting the court's action as well as other graffiti writers as an attack on the style and content, and amid intense reflection on what he wanted to do with his life, who he could trust, and who he was, Miguel wrote indelibly on his skin. He first drew a cross, a symbol of solidarity and protection that spanned across the country as well as time; later he wrote his name on his forearm. It is significant that the content of the two tattoos that he chose to get were a family symbol of support and his own name. The skin between his thumb and pointer finger on which he drew the cross was a protected space to engage in a creative practice when many other spaces were either closed or lent him little to no support. The second tattoo, his first name, was a statement, maybe to him, that he was somebody. His name meant something. It was important that Miguel chose to write his name in Old English lettering, a style that was reminiscent of a dominant world power. This style communicated control, prestige, and elitism. Here, Miguel also used tradition to form another community of practice—people, past and present, that he felt connected to in some way. It included an Anglo Saxon culture from a previous century combined with a new group of Latino youth who have appropriated the semiotic marker. Cintron uses the terms *inner-* and *outerscapes* to describe the dialectical process through which people appropriate cultural material and forms. Here he speaks in particular about the use of Old English lettering:

> Old English, as emblem of a romanticized past, allowed its purveyors to rupture the humiliation of the present. In this sense, Old English was a site for creating the stylized difference of street gang life. In appropriating this style, gangs made it their signature writ large. Moreover, Old English was part of a larger iconography that included thumpers, Too Low Flows, hair and clothing styles, and so on, each one a special site for creating an exaggeration that might be awarded respect. This iconography, then, represented a

kind of confluence in which Old English as evocation of the past blended with other styles that evoked the modern. Each style was a site that could offer the remaking of one's world—or at least a rhetorical remaking behind which lay a version of the real work, biting hard, insisting that it be made over through any means necessary. (1997, pp. 172–173)

Miguel used the canvas of his own body to relocate himself, so to speak. The cross located him within a community of people. His name, his "real" name, broadcasted, if Miguel chose to reveal it, that it ultimately could not be erased. Besides wearing a glove, Miguel was unable to conceal the cross on his hand. However, he could choose to hide his name by simply wearing a long-sleeved shirt. This was significant because, as Carlos's story of the VL reveals, family comes before the individual. Miguel applied this logic to his graffiti squads as well: "My pieces [his individual work] are nothing compared to what my people are, right, my squad." Miguel would often tell me that if he had to die for his family, he would.

CONCLUSION

A part of Miguel's life that I have only alluded to in this chapter but feel is still extremely important is the fact that he dropped out of school, having only sporadically attended during one third of the school year. To conclude this chapter, I would like to pose one possible reason for why I think he chose to not go to school and also connect the lack of school as a consistent space to Miguel's constantly shifting creative practice.

Because of Miguel's life circumstances, the middle-class notion of the need for "a room of one's own" in order to engage in creative expression simply was not an option. Unlike Ian, Miguel's bedroom and home life encouraged a different form of creative practice. He did not have the luxury of being able to step into his creative practice or leave it laying around, so to speak. Each time that he worked on his models, tied flies, or painted his boots involved time and effort to set things up and carefully put things away so that others would not interfere.

While Woolf's (1929) contention that people require personal space in order to create has a middle-class orientation, it is also a useful metaphor for thinking about the various ways in which youth need time and space to work and engage in creative practices. Miguel taught me that a room of one's own in relation to creative practice does not need to be defined or restricted by four walls. A room of one's own can be moments of time that Miguel claimed for himself to draw on his skin. Perhaps more important, a room of one's own does not need to be individualistic. A room of one's own can include other people: an inclusive space as opposed to an exclusive and singular one. Familial responsibility and other forces like poverty, the public's negative evaluation of his creative practice, and the seemingly omnipresent police force led Miguel to adapt and shift his creative work and the space on/ in which he practiced. Communities of practice, his ongoing reflection and evaluation of his life and work, his willingness to experiment, and the results of various performances influenced the trajectory and shape of his practice as well. I wonder if Miguel's school situation, of which he only talked as oppressive and meaningless, did not acknowledge or allow room for this kind of shifting form of practice as well as these ways of experimenting, reflecting, and evaluating. In other words, was the practice of reading, writing, and learning in his school framed within a middle-class ideology that Miguel saw as counter to his own beliefs and values? Was it difficult for Miguel to define or shape the kind of "room" that he needed in order to engage in reading, writing, and learning on his terms?

For Ian, the space and time of school provided a crucial focus for reflecting on his writing in order to elaborate and craft it, for gathering with others to explore and experiment within their creative practice, and for evaluating the work of others in his community of practice. These significant connections to school ran parallel to the sanctioned practices of classes or occurred in spaces outside of academic classrooms. Even though there certainly was tension between Ian's practice and the ideology of the school, the institution did accept his work in part because of the ways in which Ian's writing echoed genres of writing sanctioned within the formal curriculum. For Miguel, as for many other students living in poverty, school was a place that could be alienating to practices that are not middle class in orientation. I can imagine how difficult it must have been for Miguel to find his way in to learning within this orientation.

Ian shows us that school is significant in relation to his practice because it was a space and time that he could manipulate, organize, and use either in conjunction with the sanctioned use of school space and time or alongside it in order to explore his creative practice. Miguel's orientation to school was markedly different than Ian's. Miguel did not see school as the kind of space he could appropriate for his creative practice. School was not a space that he could mold or shape to suit his interest. While at the beginning of the research Miguel did co-opt school time and space to write graffiti with his friends, by the end, school had become a markedly different kind of place for Miguel. Even though he was not attending school at the end of the research, in his mind school was still a space that provided him a way out of his current life situation even though he acknowledged that it did not value his way of life or cultural orientation.

Amid family obligations and an urgent feeling that he needed to make money, Miguel imagined where he could be and what he could be doing instead:

Miguel: I got to plan for my future.

Leif: And what's the future?

Miguel: Getting out of here. Making some money also.

Leif: How are you going to do that?

Miguel: Try hard as shit. Do what I got to do. Stay out of trouble.

Leif: Do you remember when we sat down together last spring? I remember you. You had your book with you. You were excited about the work that you were doing. You wanted to talk about it. You gave me a mini-lesson on old school, new school. You were showing me *Confusion*. You were talking about petroglyphs. You were really interested in it. Has a change happened?

Miguel: In truth, I ain't got time for drawing nothing no more. I got to worry about school now. I want to get out. When I get done with school, I want to go to college and get done with that. Start my life the right way....Once I'm out of Philadelphia, I ain't turning back. This ain't a place to raise no family.

Leif: Why not?

Miguel: Drugs. Shootings, you know? I don't want to have to worry about one of my kids coming home and getting shot or on drugs, or selling drugs. I know one of them is going to come out like me. There's at least one kid that comes out like the father. It could be a girl or boy. It's going to come out like the parents. I don't want my kids coming out like me.

Leif: Why not?

Miguel: I've been doing some dumb shit in my life. Try to forget about it.

Leif: Are there some things about you that you want your kids to be?

Miguel: When you don't know how to do something, be determined to figure out how to do it....Don't let nobody put you down. Fight for what you believe in. Never be scared of nobody. What they can do to you, you can do to them. I'm not scared of nobody because I know, my father taught me, what they can do to you you can do right back to them. They can beat your ass. You can beat their ass. They can kill you. You can kill them. Same thing. Never be afraid of nobody. The only one you can be afraid of is God. That's the way I was raised. And always have respect for the oldest.

In this conversation, I see Miguel's class position not only influencing the kinds of creative practices he feels he can engage in, but also influencing his job future. Miguel sees both school and graffiti as fairly insignificant practices in relation to finding a job and making money. School to Miguel is a task that does not require much personal investment: "When I get done with school, I want to go to college and get done with that." Drawing is a frivolous practice, one that gets in the way of Miguel getting serious about school. In addition, Miguel did not see how the habits of mind and body within this creative practice could in any way be connected to school. Carlos talked with Miguel often about graduating and "getting out." He also peppered these conversations with ominous predictions that Miguel would not live to be 21 if he continued to live in North Philadelphia. Through these conversations and his experience in the juvenile justice system, Miguel associated graffiti along with other life choices he made with a dead-end life. Graffiti was only going to keep him from getting out and doing things he wanted to do. However, Miguel did continue to express himself creatively. He recognized that doing graffiti made him vulnerable to being criminalized by the dominant society. Tattooing, on the other hand, was safe from such social policing.

In thinking about Miguel's move away from graffiti and his desire to go back to school, one could argue that he is headed in the right direction. Miguel is choosing to not engage in a practice that is illegal while recognizing that obtaining a high school diploma has the potential of changing his life circumstances. Certainly research does show this. However, I would argue that it will be difficult for Miguel to be successful in school without an implicit pedagogical recognition of the strengths that he brings to the classroom through the practices described above as well as his class orientation to work and learning. The final chapter will offer suggestions for how to go about understanding and honoring youth like Miguel in classrooms.

3

SCRATCHING, CUTTING, AND JUGGLING
The Turntablist as 21st-Century Scholar

The life of a young turntablist is a dynamic one, involving constant practicing, persistent searching for vinyl albums, meetings with other turntablists, performing, reading about the art form, listening to varied forms of music, and seeking out opportunities to see other turntablists play. In this chapter, I tell the story of Gil, a young turntablist. I focus on four spaces through which he hones his craft: the record store, a home recording studio, a music room in his school, and his bedroom. In these spaces, Gil performs in multiple ways, experiments to see what he is capable of doing, reflects on his craft, interprets historical texts, and evaluates his performance. Like Ian and Miguel, Gil's practice moves between traditional spaces in and out of school. I will show how Gil utilizes his craft to comment on issues like racism and oppression. Gil also creates opportunities for philosophical conversations through his craft. Finally, Gil uses his craft to deepen and make more interesting the work that he is doing in school. First, I provide a brief discussion of the history of the art form.

TURNTABLISM

Turntablism, the art of manipulating vinyl records on turntables, is one of the four elements of hip-hop. Often turntablism gets conflated with DJing. Many turntablists argue that there is an important difference. The DJ's primary goal, according to these turntablists, is to maintain a constant beat for people to dance to. Turntablists use vinyl records to make new music through manipulating the source material in drastic ways. One could argue that turntablists see the record player as an instrument for making new music while DJs see it as a vehicle for playing prerecorded music.

Hip-hop began in the Bronx at a time when the area underwent dramatic and traumatic social change. The early 1960s was a time of racial unrest and economic inequity. The established African American and Hispanic communities in the Bronx of the early 1960s began to disappear with the introduction of an expressway, which cut a swath of asphalt through the Bronx and, more specifically, directly through Hispanic and African American neighborhoods. With this intrusion into their lives, people started to leave the Bronx for other boroughs like Queens. With the exodus of people the businesses followed; by 1965, the Southside of the Bronx was a picture of urban decay. Not surprisingly, without the vibrant and supportive neighborhoods of the past, both crime and unemployment rose. Soon, street gangs followed. Within this bleak picture, hip-hop was born.

Turntablism, like all the elements of hip-hop, is a distinctly youth-oriented art form. It was created by mainly African American and Puerto Rican–American youth in the mid- to late 1960s and is sustained by youth of diverse cultural and class backgrounds today. Primarily, turntablism is a form of music. Through remixing and reassembling sampled snippets of sounds, beats, and melodies on records, the turntablist creates a new piece of music (see http://www.djbattles.com/ for current audio and video clips of turntablists). Turntablism perhaps most thoroughly embodies Kress and van Leeuwen's (1996) and Street's (2000) theorizing on the multimodality of literacy. Kress and van Leeuwen define multimodality as "a range of representational modes…a range of means of meaning-making, each affecting the formation of their subjectivity" (1996, p. 39). When Gil composes on his turntables, for example, he takes a form of representation—the vinyl record—and manipulates it with turntables to produce a new sound, a new form of representation. The "interactive elements," the found sounds on records, are "made to relate" to each other in new ways, thus creating new texts and new interpretations.

For further explanation of how a turntablist works and what kind of work is produced, I defer to Sam, the poet who won Ian's poetry slam. He also happens to be a turntablist and taught me a great deal about the art form. Gil thought of Sam as a mentor. They would often get together to talk "shop" about their practice. Sam was a senior. I knew him because he used to spend time in my classroom before school started. We shared similar musical tastes. We would spend the 15 minutes or so before the bell rang swapping names of bands that we listened to at the time. Part of Sam's way of educating me on turntablism was through giving me writing he had done on his creative practice. His essay, titled "Turntable Philosophy," clearly draws the connection between turntablism, multimodality, and the act of writing:

> The DJ represents this idea of reassembly in its purest form. Pieces from the past are put together to arrive at a present purpose, thus creating the aural collage that is called the mix. In this way the turntable/mixer combination is a tool, no different in its elemental sense than the pen and paper, for they provide a means to pull "words" and "quotes" from records and place them in a consistently new and different context. The idea of turntable language may seem farfetched, but when the roots of the language are examined, it is seen that it was not only an essential, but inevitable part of the guerrilla-art social reaction (i.e., that of Black America), similar to the origins of many arts and humanities.

Sam suggests that manipulating records is a form of language. There is the interpretation of words. There is the fashioning of a message out of these words, phrases, and sentences that have been captured from other sources. The turntablist's "referencing" of words and phrases and the manipulation of preexisting words and notes on record resemble the way in which teachers expect students to quote from the work of scholars within their essays, for example. In addition, the sampling of phrases from various albums in order to construct a new text reminds me of the way in which Shakespeare "borrowed" themes from Ovid to write his plays. Like writers of more traditional texts, turntablists make meaning out of language and ideas they did not create or conceive. Sam also mentions that turntablism is a means of social action. Turntablists create music in part to subvert the status quo or to challenge norms. We will see this in Gil's work later in the chapter.

While rap still garners all the media attention within hip-hop culture, the turntablist is back in style now and in high demand. One only needs to watch television for an hour or so to see the influence of turntablism on our broader society. Zima ads feature turntablists. Lee Jeans and Gap ads use turntablists. IKEA catalogues represent posh adolescent bedrooms with two turntables and a mixer. MTV had a turntablist how-to show. The Internet contains hundreds if not thousands of turntable Web sites.

The creative practice is global as well. There is the International Turntable Federation (ITF). This organization and others host international turntable competitions, including Disco Music Competitions (DMCs) and the ITF World Championships. Even jazz artists like Steve

Coleman and Medeski, Martin, and Wood record with turntablists as part of their bands, not to mention all of the popular bands that include sampled sounds of someone scratching. Turntablists like Q-Bert, DJ Shadow, and DJ Swamp have attained rock star status with many youth. Gil is a product of this renewed interest in the art form, and it is informing what he reads, the messages he chooses to "write" on his turntables, and how he works and learns in his everyday life.

I would like to illustrate through four vignettes the ways in which Gil works in his chosen creative practice. These glimpses into the ways he works on his turntables highlight how performance, interpretation, evaluation, experimentation, and communities of practice work together to enable Gil to be a turntablist while also having the potential to influence how work and learning are conducted in classrooms.

BECOMING A TURNTABLIST

Over the course of the research, Gil and I spent a lot of time at his house. I would sit at the edge of his bed or on the floor and he would spin for me, showing me the latest moves he was working on or taking me through a guided tour of the recent vinyl he found. Eventually, after listening to him spin for an hour or more, he would stop and we would talk about what he was up to with his turntables. During one of these conversations, Gil told me the story of how his interest piqued for turntablism and in the process illuminated for me the significance of a community of practice within this particular kind of creative practice:

> In seventh grade, Henry, he asked me about [turntablism]. I don't know how I knew so much about it. I guess I had, not really realizing it, taken an interest in it. And he asked me about it and I just told him…you play a phrase from one record and then, I know about a cross-fader somehow, and then you switch it over to the other side and let that play. Meanwhile you are rewinding the other record… and he was like, "Yo, that's so cool, I'm going to buy some [turntables]." I'm like, "That's not a bad idea." But I was interested in a lot, like guitar, spending money on that. I couldn't ask for more stuff because I was still developing those skills….Eventually, I bought them, I think it was the end of eighth grade. I bought [Henry's] turntables because he had moved on to paintball…he wanted to get a more expensive gun so I bought his turntables from him and I learned on them, and the first needle broke the second night. So I had been learning on a mixer and one turntable for half a year at least.…It was cool just to have turntables. Then he asked for them back to sell them.…I had money from working at the camp

so I go to this place on 9th and Market and the guys there were pretty nice....I told them that I was starting out, and they're like, "All right, we'll give you that coffin case, two xl500," which are direct drive which was the main thing that I was looking for, "646 scratch mixer," which is really nice, "and whatever small things you want, stylus or whatever." I was like, "OK." He was like, "For $500."...I only had enough for the turntables. So my mom was like, "Why don't you just get the turntables now?" I was like, "Fine, I will." She was like, "Wait. Give me what's in your pockets." So I just gave her this big wad of cash and she's like, "Just get the whole thing." So I got the whole package....From there, I had two turntables. I was dangerous...I see that as really the beginning. The stuff in seventh grade and eighth grade led up to that, but I really couldn't start the idea of turntablism because the whole idea of turntablism is the creation of music and you can't really create with [one turntable] because when you are manipulating there really isn't anything supporting it or behind it.

Gil's interest in the art form started through a conversation with his friend. Through that conversation, Gil realized the tacit knowledge he had on the subject. Somehow, perhaps through the music he listened to, his group of friends, and the ubiquity of hip-hop, turntablism was a part of his life. Before showing Henry what he knew about turntablism, the art form lurked somewhere in the background of Gil's life. It took this conversation, and others, for Gil to recognize his interest in it. But at the time, he was busy with learning how to play guitar. This work involved more than time. It also involved money. So the time and resources for pursuing turntablism did not become available until almost a year later. He scrounged up the money through summer work and bought his friend's turntables. A developing community of practice, including his friend Henry, provided Gil with the resources he needed to get started.

However, as Gil states, the early work he did on this system really did not amount to turntablism to him. It took making money through a job for the intended purpose of buying turntables, a journey to a renowned music store for turntablists and DJs, and some financial help from his mom in order for him to buy a system that he felt represented the beginning of his real work as a turntablist. This system involved more than a mixer and "direct drive" turntables. It also involved a certain kind of stylus and slipmats—both standard yet important accessories for any turntablist. Through this material culture, Gil was able to do the work of a turntablist—the creation of music through the manipulation of records. However, becoming a turntablist is more than having the raw materials. In the section that follows, I show how Gil's use of particular spaces associated with turntablism influenced his interest in and development of this creative practice as well.

Cue Records

One of the central spaces for the practice of turntablism is the record store. The record store is the source of the vinyl needed to compose on turntables. Turntablists spend hours digging, like archaeologists, through stacks of records to find unusual and rare vinyl with which to create new musical pieces.

Two days before Christmas, I had the opportunity to go "graverobbing" with Gil. Turntablists use the term "graverobbing" to describe the process of searching for rare and old vinyl at used record stores. Gil wanted to go to Cue Records, a fairly new record store devoted to turntablism. The store had six long racks of vinyl, most of the record jackets protected by plastic covers. The essential gear of a turntablist—shoulder bags for holding records, t-shirts and baseball caps with the names of underground record companies emblazoned on them, and turntable slipmats—lined the wall. Posters of new groups and musical icons like Miles Davis and Charlie Parker hung on the walls. Interspersed between these racks were turntables. At the time Gil and I were there, several other youth stood at these turntables, lifting the needles and putting them back down on the records, turning the albums over, reading the labels, listening to see if they wanted to purchase them, bobbing their heads to the beats.

Gil started his search for records in the stacks of new vinyl. He ran his hands over rows of records, stopping every now and then to look at one that caught his eye. Gil had his heart set on *Shaolin*, an album filled with martial arts sounds, but Cue did not have it. The *whoops* and *smacks* of martial arts sound effects make for excellent scratches, Gil informed me. By manipulating the speed at which the record spins, turntablists can alter the tone of a scream or whoop. Those who are particularly skilled can reproduce other songs—the well-known theme from Beethoven's Fifth Symphony, for example—entirely out of such a sound effect. Turntablists use the smacks from these soundtracks to create beats for their pieces.

He spent a lot of time in the hip-hop section, listening to records. Every now and then he would say a name aloud, "Miles Davis," or he would ask me a question: "Which is the most recent Skratch Piklz album?" He mentioned that he had heard of certain records before, pulling them out and showing them to me. I pulled out a few, including the soundtrack to *Enter the Dragon*. Gil listened to it and then evaluated it, saying, "The organ's great, but there's not enough sound effects."

After digging for a good 45 minutes, we went down to the used records in the basement. They were arranged in a loose order—break beats, soundtracks, sound effects, hip-hop, rock, etc. In these stacks I found three records for Gil that I thought he would be interested in: a counting and alphabet record, a Disney folk record, and a Disney record of famous film songs. Gil took them over to a turntable and listened to each one, dropping the needle in certain places, reading the liner notes of the record jackets. After listening to all three, Gil said that he was going to buy the famous film songs because they would sound amazing with a beat behind them. Gil listened to some other records, mostly of break beats, but did not like any of them.

When Gil checked out, the woman working at the store asked him if he would like to be on the mailing list. That way he would get information about promotions, etc. He gave her his e-mail address. She told him that from now on, when he came in, he should give that address and that would be his account. She also picked up the X-ecutioners album that Gil intended to buy and said, "This is a great album." He smiled and nodded in agreement.

The importance of Cue in terms of Gil's practice cannot be underestimated. It was a space dedicated to his creative practice. Within this space, Gil immersed himself in the argot of the practice as well as the aesthetic. He was surrounded by the material culture from which turntablists make their music. The argot was reinforced through word of mouth as well as print. Gil heard it and read it on the labels that defined particular kinds of records. Being in this space also afforded Gil the chance to see how others within the larger community of practice of turntablism practiced. The turntables that lined the main shop floor were like ministages in a way, where Gil could see other turntablists perform. He could watch their techniques—the way they moved their hands, how they used the cross-fader on the mixer, the way in which they wore the headphones on their heads—as well as see the kinds of records that they selected to play. Finally, when Gil purchased records, he received validation from the woman at the counter and access to what could be argued was a more exclusive group within the community of practice: the Cue Records accountholders. This positive evaluation and institutional acceptance were subtle and important recognitions that Gil knew what he was doing in terms of this creative practice and that he had good taste.

Building a Community of Practice: The
Significance of Social Relations

While driving home from Cue Records, Gil talked about the different people who influenced his turntable work. Gil explained to me
that his main DJ influence at the time was Mix Master Mike. Mix
Master Mike is known for his unusual blending of found sounds and
snippets of dialogue. A newspaper article described his style as "less
a showcase of turntable expertise than a surreal glimpse into a bril-
liantly spaced-out mind. Beats break down and recombine into new
patterns; rhythms swerve, shift, and reverse. Snippets of dialogue
from sci-fi films stutter percussively over a panoply of scratches:
forwards, scribbles, tears, chirps, tear-chirps." Mix Master Mike
describes his own work as "turntabling in a musical way. When you
do mix tapes, you blend other people's music, but a musician makes
his own....I made all the beats on the album, and I'm scratching
out everything—a horn, a violin, conga drums—so it sounds like an
actual band."

Many youth know Mix Master Mike through his work with the
Beastie Boys, a genre-bending rap group from New York. However, Mix
Master Mike has also made a name for himself through his work with a
turntable group, an interesting community of practice, called the Invisible Skratch Piklz, as well as his own solo work. The Invisible Skratch
Piklz dominated the DMC three years running and was asked to stop
competing in order to allow other artists to win.

Gil included Sam in his community of practice as well. He was quick
to point out that Sam was not an influence because of the way he played.
Rather, Sam influenced Gil through the conversations they had about
music and turntablism. Gil told me that he and Sam would often meet
after school and spin together. During one of these practice sessions,
Sam told him that it was a good sign that he could do so much on the
system that he had, implying that it was not the easiest set of components with which to work. During this particular session, Sam gave
Gil the chance to spin on his Technic 1200s—the industry standard
for turntablism. From that conversation and practice time, Gil said he
planned to save up for Technic 1200s.

Gil also talked about a friend of his who spun as well and who was
the only other person with whom Gil practiced on a regular basis.
He said that simple things Gil could do on the turntables fascinated
his friend. Gil hissed and said, "He doesn't practice at all and doesn't
really understand the art." He continued, laughing, "One time he said
that he would like to win the DMC some day, like it was no big deal."

I asked Gil why he continued to spin with him, and he informed me that this friend was a good source for vinyl. Gil explained that they would often swap albums that they bought. This increased the content of Gil's vinyl collection considerably and broadened the range of music that he could pull from to play. I also got the sense that Gil appreciated the positive feedback that he received from this friend, even if he did not consider him to be a legitimate turntablist, similar to the way Ian appreciated the encouragement he received from Abe and his sister regarding his poetry.

Gil mentioned that he overheard one of the music teachers talking with another teacher about Gil's turntables. This music teacher told another teacher that Gil used the turntables like an instrument. Gil took this as a compliment, thinking that he had in some way influenced this teacher in his way of thinking about turntables and music. What I found particularly interesting about this story was how this music teacher legitimated Gil's work on the turntables through connecting it to a sanctioned creative practice. In other words, the music teacher was able to see the worth of Gil's playing because of the way in which it resembled a musician playing a standard musical instrument.

The different people within this disparate community of practice, of whom Gil spoke above, served different purposes in his work. Mix Master Mike along with the Skratch Piklz create music that Gil wished to emulate on one level, but he also pulled from Mix Master Mike's stylings to create his own "type" of music as I will show later. Sam, on the other hand, provided a space for talking about and reflecting on their craft. Within these conversations, they discussed techniques. However, these talks also involved discussing all different kinds of music, books, and movies. These kinds of media influence the art of turntablism, evidenced from the kinds of records available at Cue. Gil's connection with Sam also created a safe space for evaluation and encouragement.

Encouragement came in different forms from different people for Gil. Peer feedback played a role. It was important to have peers who were amazed at what he did. Because of the subcultural nature of turntablism, the negative feedback was important too because it provided a way for knowing whether or not he was too mainstream. Conversely, it was also important that the music teacher validated his craft as a form of music, bringing it into the realm of sanctioned artistic work. At the same time, I think it was Gil's ability to convince the music teacher of turntablism's validity through his playing that was the most important part of that interaction.

PLAYING AT SCHOOL: TURNTABLISM AS PERFORMATIVE, EXPERIMENTAL, REFLECTIVE, AND INTERPRETIVE

Through the jazz teacher's generosity, Gil and other students interested in turntablism had a room off of the main music room where they could set up their equipment, practice, and record together. It was through this space that Gil and others were able to transport their out-of-school creative practices into school. The room was a popular place at the end of the day. The sound of needles scratching vinyl always drew a crowd. Within this space, Gil had the opportunity to observe other turntablists at work, to share his playing with others, to talk about turntablism as art and craft, and to use his skills to think about and comment on his own life experiences.

This small room off of the jazz room had several tables of equipment. One held two turntables and a mixer in between. A sampler and drum machine faced the turntables. There were also a four-track machine and tape recorder. Facing all of this equipment was an electronic keyboard. All of this material rested on top of an old Persian rug. A mic stand stood at the ready to the right of the four-track machine. The rest of the room was filled with a worn Victorian-style couch, a baby grand piano, and a fairly new computer with a laser printer. Bookshelves, haphazardly stocked with all kinds of records and sheet music, lined the walls. Posters of the films *Goodfellas* and *The Godfather* hung on the walls. Other posters included a *Superfly* movie poster, a poster of Bob Marley smoking a large joint, a poster of Tupac Shakur, and one black-light print of two people standing on a mountain with their arms raised.

On this particular day, Del, a senior and mentor for Gil, sat behind the table that held his turntables. He was rapping to a beat, half to himself. When Del saw us, he took the headphones off his ears, rested them around his neck, and said, "What's up?" Gil walked over to him, shook his hand, and introduced me. Del nodded at me. He then asked, "You want to listen to the intro to the album?" Gil nodded, "Definitely."

Del turned around to the DAT player and put in the tape. The intro blasted an aural collage of phrases from recent rap albums out of the speaker to the side of the turntables: *My sound surrounds you like racism. You feel it all around you.* The three of us stood and nodded to the beat, making sounds of agreement when we recognized particular phrases or rappers: *I'm trying to catch my people in all different stages, all different phases.* No phrase was repeated: *If knowledge is the key then show me the lock.* Each blended seamlessly into the next. At the end of the intro, which was about two minutes long, both Gil and I said, "Damn." Del smiled. I asked, "How long did it take to put that together?" Del sighed, "Over eight hours."

Del checked the clock and realized that he had to go. Gil pointed to his turntables: "Can I spin for a while?" Del said, "Sure, just take care of my babies and put away any albums you use." On the way out the door, he added, "And, yo, don't let anyone else mess with them, OK?" Gil put the headphones on and said, "Promise." With that, Del left. Gil told me that this was usually what he did: went up to this room and played for hours before catching up with his friends at around 6.

As Gil warmed up, by experimenting with scratching various phrases on two albums that he found in the stack of vinyl on the floor, we talked about the ubiquity of turntablism in the media. I sat on the couch and asked, "You ever see that Zima ad where that dude is spinning at a party so intensely that the records on the decks melt?" At this point in the ad, the turntablist picks up a Zima that miraculously cools everything off and he is able to get back to spinning records. Gil winced. "That ad's corny: corny because Zima is corny and because Zima has nothing to do with hip-hop." He added, "Zima's not advertising with turntablism because they care about hip-hop. They're just out to make money." Gil, like Sam, felt strongly that playing on his turntables was in part a political act. Honing his craft helped sustain hip-hop as a cultural form that avoided commodification. The commercial, on the other hand, was only capitalizing on the rising popularity of the art form with no recognition of its roots and cultural significance. Through ads like this one, turntablism ran the risk of merely being a product.

About a half hour into spinning, he looked up from the turntables and said, "Guess I'm not going to practice." I asked him what he meant. Gil said, "I was supposed to go to track practice." The conference championships were this weekend, and the team was traveling to the track to check it out. Gil did not seem too concerned about missing what sounded like a fairly important practice. I asked, "You want to run and catch the bus?" He shrugged, said, "Nah," and went back to the turntables.

A few minutes later, three longhaired eighth-grade boys came in and lounged on the couch to listen to Gil play. One of them leaned against the table, "Can I spin? Gil? Gil? Gil?" Gil smirked and shook his head no. With this audience, Gil performed the physicality of a turntablist. He put the headphones on and rested them on his temples when he was not using them. When checking for a phrase on a record, he would hold one earphone to his ear with his shoulder. At one point, the eighth grader who wanted to use the turntables said half-sarcastically, "Gil! I love you!" as Gil played. He smiled.

Students would drift in and out of the space, sometimes staying for only a few minutes, other times hanging out for an hour or so. When the eighth graders eventually left, two seniors entered the room and flopped down onto the couch. Gil was experimenting with several albums that he had recently acquired. The first one was titled *Mr. Nosy,* a children's novelty record that contained minimorality plays. He sampled phrases like "must try harder" and "the police." He manipulated one of the records on the turntables to maintain a consistent beat as he scratched phrases on the other album. Gil looked over at me while experimenting with the beat he found and said, "Sounds like a car chase." It was subversive. He smiled, "Runnin', like evading the law." The seniors nodded in agreement. Other students drifted in while he played. They sat down on the sofa and nodded to this beat. Sometimes they would laugh at phrases Gil selected to scratch. Other times they would walk over to the table and watch Gil spin.

In the midst of this activity, Gil and I, and the two seniors who had come in earlier, talked about the ability of the turntablist to, in the words of one of the seniors, "tell a new story out of one that already exists." For example, Gil experimented with the soundtrack to *The Rescuers,* a children's movie from the 1970s about two mice that rescue an orphaned girl from an abusive woman, and he scratched certain phrases that created a completely different story from the original.

Later, I asked the two seniors and Gil, "Why are the samples that you pick so interesting when you take them out of context?" This came up while Gil spun the soundtrack to *Raiders of the Lost Ark.* While experimenting with various voices and sounds on the album, Gil found the sound of a gunshot. Through scratching this sound, he transformed the gunshot into a drumbeat. Through the experimental freedom of reappropriating this sound, Gil took a dominant discourse (gunshot as violent act) and invested it with his own particular inflection (gunshot as rhythm). One senior suggested, "It's the timing of the phrases." The art of phrasing to him was the element of surprise, catching the listener off guard with a quirky or familiar pop culture reference or found sound. The other senior added, "You got to be able to kinda recognize where the sample's coming from or from what kind of music." The comfort of the familiar makes it possible for the listener to, perhaps, suspend his or her disbelief and create an alternative reality of sorts and to take pleasure in recognizing a familiar sound, voice, passage, or beat juxtaposed with another sound, voice, passage, or beat from a disparate source. For example, at one point, Gil scratched the phrase "Sunday school," playing it over and over again. By taking this easily recognized idea in the form of a phrase out of context, and placing it within the context of that music room at that moment in time, Gil essentially made the familiar strange. He suggested, "Sampling's a lot like wearing a Sesame Street t-shirt to high school. You're fucking around with what's expected of you."

In considering the applicability of Gil's craft as illustrated within this vignette to teaching, there are several points I wish to make. First, the kind of work that Gil enjoys to do on his own time is highly experimental and it involves working to create something original. Second, there is also a subversive quality to it: the recognition that the composition challenges normative behavior or language use contributes to the desire to practice and play for others. Third, notice too that the practice of being a turntablist at times involves performing in a semipublic space. This semipublic space makes possible the occasional reflective conversation that rises out of the work, a pause to either think about what has been playing or to consider what the most recent composition means. Fourth, work within this realm involves others coming up and looking closely at what Gil is doing, not necessarily to judge him, but instead to watch him work. They want to see the way he uses his hands, to understand the effect that he is making, and to check to see the album he decides to play. Finally, the everyday practice of a turntablist involves working in spaces where multiple things happen at once. People are listening, watching, talking to each other and the turntablist, and flowing in and out of the space. It is this multiplicity that contributes to the vitality of the creative practice.

Toward the end, once the seniors left, just Gil and I remained with the hum of the amps in the background. Gil said he wanted to play a song for me. "Have you heard 'E Pluribus Unum' by The Last Poets?" He pulled the vinyl out from the record jacket. I told him that I had. Gil smiled and placed it gently on the platter of the left turntable. He placed the needle on the outer edge of the record. The popping and hissing of a well-worn record filled the room.

At the time, as we sat and listened to this song together, the anger and frustration of the lyrics did not register with me nearly as powerfully as they do now with the advantage of hindsight. In the midst of listening to the song, I was swept away by the raw and minimal beat. I "heard" the lyrics, but not as deeply as I think Gil wanted me to. When the song ended, Gil only said that he agreed with a lot of what they said and proceeded to put away the albums much like someone would reshelve books in a library. I was struck by the image of Gil putting the records away and did not ask him to explain what he meant about agreeing with the song.

Thinking about the song now, hearing the beat only faintly in my head, and knowing Gil the way that I do now, I think I understand more clearly why he wanted to play me that song at that particular time in that particular place. I hear the way the song resonated with Gil, how it had a context beyond just being an interesting piece of music. Finally, I see how the turntable can be a place for Gil to be reflective and construct an interpretation of his current life situation through an important piece of hip-hop history.

The Last Poets brutally deconstruct the dollar bill, showing how money has corrupted those in power and how those in power—white men—have oppressed African Americans. It is not a particularly new idea now, but the message of the song—originally recorded in 1972—is fresh to me because of the way they deconstruct the text and images on the dollar bill. The Last Poets take each image and each word and explain its significance and culpability in the history of oppression in America: *so the people don't get any in the land of the plenty*. Finally, what is perhaps the most powerful and lasting image of this song for me is the way in which The Last Poets show how racism is ingrained, even printed, in our society. The way money is used can be oppressive, they argue, but what is even more sinister is how images and text can be used to weave racism into the infrastructure of society.

In the music room, listening to the song that day, the lyrics of this diatribe against racial and economic injustice poured out of the speakers and slid underneath the door into the second-story hallway of the auditorium that is part of the campus of an upper-middle-class, predominantly white private institution. By the time the lyrics made their way down to the end of the hall, they were probably faint, the message indecipherable to a group of students who may have been sitting on the faded Oriental rug. However, through Gil's act of playing the song in this room, the lyrics were now a part of this institution. I interpret Gil's playing of this song as an interpretation of the subtle and not-so-subtle racism that he experienced at this school.

Gil came across this song *through* his work as a turntablist. He heard about The Last Poets from other hip-hop that he listened to as well as from other turntablists talking about the music that influenced them. He read about them in liner notes on albums in his collection. Gil learned through his practice that they are an important part of the lineage of hip-hop. By playing them, Gil signified his knowledge of their significance and in a way authenticated that he *was* a turntablist. He also connected his current life situation with the life experience of his hip-hop "ancestry."

About a year before we sat in that space off from the music room, listening to "E Pluribus Unum," Gil and I worked on a different research project. In this project, Gil and I explored the concept of inscribed and chosen identities in his high school. In the process of working on this project, Gil shared with me that there were times when he felt he needed to prove himself academically as a young black man in a predominantly white school. As a way of explaining this feeling, he sent me this e-mail:

> I always feel the need to prove myself…I was in the bathroom… Chris walks in, and says hi…Then out of the clear blue sky he says "All of the black teachers in this school were hired because they are black." Now I know that Chris is something of a mathematical genius, but his social skills are horrible…I don't want to prove to him that they are qualified, because its not so much what he said, but what it revealed about what he is thinking…One time I said to Dan [a friend of Gil's] "I think I might have gotten a 100 on the lit test." Right away two guys come over and ask me if I want to bet. They both bet $5, and even though I stay away from gambling, I took their money. Now if that's not having to prove myself I don't know what is.

Gil jumps to a conclusion in this story that the two guys who question whether or not he aced the test were in fact implying that because Gil was black, he could not have possibly scored that high. They could have just been teasing him like they would any other student or friend, regardless of his or her race. However, Gil's response to their taunt is indicative of the social climate in which we live. It is powerful and quite frustrating to think that regardless of the two students' motives, in the back of Gil's mind was the possibility that they were being discriminatory, and because of that, he had to respond defensively to prove his worth or intelligence.

Imagine for a moment the two incidents that Gil mentions in the e-mail above somehow being in that room on the day when Gil played "E Pluribus Unum" for me. Perhaps they were in his head when he put down the needle. The song speaks to the discrimination and oppression present in those two stories. It makes me think of the money that exchanged hands in the story that Gil told in the e-mail. Like in the song, money in Gil's story was used as a vehicle for forcing Gil to prove that what he said was true. The money was a mechanism for placing the two white students in a position of power over Gil. Through laying down $5 each, they were in the position of being able to judge whether or not Gil was right. I would argue that Gil played "E Pluribus Unum" in part to tell the story of incidents like this where issues of race, class, and power put Gil in the position of constantly negotiating his identity. It was an act of witnessing in a way. Playing the song provided Gil a way of interpreting feelings, thoughts, and ideas that were swirling around in his head at the time. The turntable concretized those feelings, thoughts, and ideas.

Gil worked on the turntables for a good three hours on that day after school. In that time, he performed his skills on the turntables to those who came in. Instead of a formal performance, it was a series of mini/in-process performances where Gil experimented with new moves to see the reaction he would get. He also reflected with other turntablists in the room about his practice, exploring with others why he does what he does, what hip-hop means to him, and why turntablism intrigues people. Finally, Gil used his turntables to interpret a particular song within the context of his life. On the way out I asked him if spending this much time in the room was normal and he said, "Definitely. One time my mom got so pissed at me because I was here until, like, 7:30."

UNCOMMON SPACES IN THE PRACTICE OF TURNTABLISM

While the spaces directly associated with Gil's turntablism—the record store and the music room, for example—are essential for practicing and refining his craft, over the year and a half I spent with Gil, I noticed that other spaces that I would not have originally associated with his creative practice played significant roles in Gil's utilization of the five habits of mind and body that energize his work and learning as a turntablist. These spaces include his church, his school's jazz band, and an acquaintance's home recording studio.

Church

During the research, Gil infrequently attended church. He would go to youth group meetings and play with the church house band. On one evening that I went to church with Gil, he was to play with the band for an event that celebrated the youth who were a part of the congregation.

The church was large and low-roofed. Ms. Hendrix, Gil's mother, told me that it was only a few years old. Inside, the sanctuary must have been able to fit more than a thousand people. Pews with individual seats extended far back to the rear of the sanctuary. There was a stage in front with six microphones for singers. A discrete podium sat in the center of this stage. The house musicians played to the left of the stage. There were a keyboard and drum kit. When we entered the sanctuary, a young man practiced on the drums. Gil immediately went over to the musicians "pit" and started setting up his amp and guitar.

I sat down with Gil's mother and her friend and watched Gil set up. As people found seats, they waved to others they knew and nodded a greeting to still others. Many said hello with a hug. Several youth came in after Gil carrying instruments of various kinds: drums, horns, guitars. Once the sanctuary filled with people, a woman took the stage and spoke into the microphone at the podium. She looked out over the crowd and said:

> This evening we're all about praising the Lord. We're going to praise him with the stringed instruments and we're going to praise him with the organ, and we don't have a harp so we will have to substitute that with the piano. But we are very happy that the Lord has put so many people with gifts in our church family.

With that introduction, the woman opened up the musical event. In between individual performances by violinists, pianists, and drummers, the house band played hymns that the audience sang, led by the woman who opened the evening. While the band played, Gil kept a close eye on the woman playing the keyboard in the house band. She led the group and showed Gil the chord changes for the songs. After several songs in which Gil followed the lead of the keyboardist, he stepped back from the piano and began experimenting a bit, soloing over the melody. The leader smiled her approval. Later in the show, the bandleader took the stage and introduced Gil to the audience:

> We are very blessed this evening that we are joined by a member of our fellowship that we were not even aware of how talented he was or that he was in our midst. And he was playing already this evening. His name is Gil Hendrix. He's playing the guitar, and he looks to be with us for many, many more days. Gil.

The audience gave him a boisterous round of applause. And Gil met the applause with a gracious bow over his guitar, a slight wave, and a smile.

This evening provided a space for Gil to experiment on his guitar with the support of the house band. At first, he learned the discourse of the group, so to speak, following the chord progressions of the song, not straying at all from the way in which the song was written. Through this form of "legitimate peripheral participation," Gil then became comfortable later in the performance to take risks and improvise off of the melody of the song being performed (Lave & Wenger, 1991).

This event also provided a chance for Gil to see other youth at creative work, similar to the way Ian watched other spoken word artists perform at the Painted Bride and the slam that he organized at his school. Gil sat on the stage steps and watched as fellow youth performed original pieces for drums, violin, piano, and voice. One performance in particular stirred the already energetic audience into a frenzy. It was a duo of two drummers. The woman emceeing the event introduced the young men, saying, "We're lucky to have two brothers here who play the drums. Welcome them." The audience clapped, and suddenly, from the rear of the sanctuary came the sound of a drum, banging out a contagious beat. And then another drum joined him, making the original beat even more complicated with a counterrhythm. People in the audience craned their necks and turned their whole bodies around in the pews to see the two brothers slowly walking their way up the two side aisles of the sanctuary, banging on drums hanging from their necks. The beat filled the sanctuary to the point that you could not hear anything else.

The audience got into the performance, clapping along to the rhythm and smiling. Once the two brothers made it to the stage, they turned with military precision and walked toward one another. When they met in the center of the stage, they then turned toward the audience, banged out one last verse of the beat, and stopped together on time, tight. The audience rivaled the loudness and energy of the drums with their applause afterward. When the applause died down, the taller brother took the microphone and said, "Hello. How is everyone doing tonight?"

The audience responded with "Good!"

"All right," he said. "We named this first piece 'Genesis' because God created heaven and earth, and we created this beat." The audience laughed and applauded in agreement and the two brothers smiled. Then the two brothers launched into the second beat. The taller brother started the beat. Both faced the crowd. It is difficult to put into words the sound of the drums. The two brothers worked the entire drum, not just relying on the center; they played the sides of the drums and the sticks themselves. They were always together, reading each other for changes in the rhythm. The true sign of the effort and time that it took to do this kind of work was evident in the ease with which they made it look.

At the end of this second piece, the emcee took the stage and said,

> Good thing we caught them before their world tour. We are so proud of these two young men. I first heard them in a youth service several months ago, and their growth in that amount of time has been tremendous so we thank the Lord for them, for the support they get from their families that enables them to play.

Jazz Band

Gil also played his guitar in the jazz band at school. This jazz band was renowned for tackling particularly difficult pieces and putting on stunning performances. The jazz band teacher, Mr. Talbot, was a favorite of the students. When not teaching, Mr. Talbot played with leading jazz musicians in the area. The last time I saw him, he told me of his trip to India with Steve Coleman, a progressive jazz musician, and his band.

Every spring, the jazz band performed with the other musical groups of the school. The jazz band performed toward the end to keep the audience there. The administration learned early that when the jazz band played close to the beginning of the lineup, a considerable portion of the audience left. The spring concert was always special because it was the time when the various groups honor and say good-bye to the senior members.

For this concert, Gil asked several people to come: his mother, his mother's sister and husband, his grandparents, a coworker, and me. As the jazz band members set up their equipment, Mr. Talbot took centerstage, looked out over the crowd, and said, in his quiet voice, "We are all in for something special tonight." I leaned forward, straining to hear what he said. "Tonight, you are going to see students working together to make amazing music." He went on to explain that the youth who made up the band were at different skill levels. Rather than seeing this disparity in skill as detrimental, Mr. Talbot said it made the music more interesting. "There will be times when you will need to listen carefully for the beauty, but it is there."

In the middle of the first song, the drummer, bassist, and piano player completely changed the tempo of the music, something that they had never done before, Gil later told me. After this song, Mr. Talbot stood up and praised the members of the band for taking that risk. He then talked about how the band was like a secret society. They practiced early on Friday mornings. Their goal was to work to a point where people could experiment and make spontaneous music. At another point in the show, the senior piano player passed the honor of playing in the band to a sophomore by playing a duet together. For most of this performance, Gil sat off to the side, watching while the seniors played, like he was waiting in the wings for his turn.

When it came time for him to play his solo, he took centerstage and worked up and down the fretboard along to the incredibly complex rhythm of the "Tao of Mad Phat" by Steve Coleman. He bent over the guitar. His head rocked back and forth to the decisions he made on the fretboard. The trumpet player said something to him as he took Gil's place centerstage for the next solo—a recognition that he had done something amazing.

After this song, Mr. Talbot talked about how seniors needed to remember what it was like to play when they were freshmen, and people needed to remember that things do not get easy when you become a senior. It is all hard work. He talked about what beautiful music the band played and how well they played together. There was a discourse of tradition, legacy, talent, and passion for music.

The Studio

While researching Gil's practice as a turntablist, I had the chance to spend an evening with him at a home recording studio. Gil had met a guy named Rudolpho at the local grocery store where they both worked. Somehow the two started talking about music one day and Gil told Rudolpho that he was a turntablist. The story goes, as told by Gil, that Rudolpho did not know much about turntablism and asked if Gil wanted to come by his home studio sometime to jam.

Rudolpho's house was on a side street off of a main arterial road that separated the Main Line from Philadelphia. Rows of white bilevel 1950s homes lined the street. When I pulled up to Rudolpho's house, I was not sure anyone was home. All of the blinds were shut. I walked up the two short flights of concrete steps and knocked on the screen door.

A woman who appeared to be in her 60s answered. I asked her if Gil was there. She looked at me with a puzzled expression and then recognition slowly changed the contours of her face. She smiled and then called out over her shoulder, "Rudolpho?"

Rudolpho came out from what I assumed to be his bedroom. A short, stocky guy, with the build of a gymnast, Rudolpho smiled, said, "Thanks, Ma," and shook my hand. He then told me Gil was not there yet. He suggested I come back and wait for Gil with him in the studio.

Rudolpho showed me back to the room from which he came. It was a small room, maybe 8 by 8 feet, literally packed with recording equipment. In the center of this room was a 24-track mixer that left only about 3 feet of space to get by. There was an electronic piano against one wall, along with his computer. An older Moog synthesizer took up another wall. Gray, dimpled sound-dampening material lined most of the walls and ceiling. After being amazed at the amount of stuff in this small room, I asked Rudolpho, "How do you fit a band in here?" He laughed and said, "We get creative. I usually end up using my bedroom." He nodded toward the adjoining small room. My attention was immediately drawn to the military precision with which the bed was made and the teddy bear that rested in the center of the pillow.

Rudolpho was in his early 20s. As a child, he had sung in the Philadelphia Boys' Choir but told me that he enjoyed playing music more than singing. He graduated from a nearby university with a major in music theory. He now lived at home. He wanted to make a career out of producing but said that right now he could not make enough money doing it.

It was around this time that Gil came in, carrying his guitar and amplifier. He said, "What's up?" and looked for a place to put his gear down. After shaking hands with Rudolpho and me, and spending a few minutes plugging in the equipment, Gil and Rudolpho launched into a prolonged session of experimenting and improvising on the musical instruments. Gil started out on his guitar. Rudolpho sat down at his piano. I managed to find a corner where I could wedge myself into a chair. Rudolpho flicked on the drum machine that laid out a standard 4/4 beat. Gil asked, "Do you have anything funkier?" Rudolpho moved through the prerecorded beats until he found one to Gil's liking, and then they started playing. The music filled the tiny room.

The experimental playing was enhanced by occasional conversations between Gil and Rudolpho. These conversations seemed to serve several purposes. For example, at one point while the two jammed, Rudolpho asked Gil if he was just making up what he was playing on the guitar, which started a discussion on why they liked the beat and how it blended with their playing:

Rudolpho: Are you just doing that on improv or is there a reason why you are using a flat nine?

Gil: Just like the groove. I mean, I like it, but it fits with the groove.

Rudolpho: Yeah because it's going down. I see. I see.

Gil: It's going down a half step [Gil shows him on his guitar].

Rudolpho: Do you change the minor to a major or do you just keep it the same?

Gil: No, I usually keep it the same.

Rudolpho: OK.

Gil: Just because for some reason it stays more stable.

They continued to play together. Rudolpho fiddled around in a flat nine. After a few more minutes of playing, he asked Gil what chords he was using.

Gil: There's a seventh. To a sharp nine and a flat tenth.

Rudolpho: [trying it out on his keyboard] So the nine would be sharp, so it would be a tenth, I see. So that's actually the third of the chord though.

Gil: Yeah, yeah, yeah.

Rudolpho: Because you have the C. So A minor seventh…
Gil: Third, seventh…
Rudolpho: Plus the seventh. That's a really nice sound. It makes the whole thing sound nice and thick. I was wondering what that was.
Gil: Also, since the harmonic minor scale goes down a half-step [shows it on his guitar] since there are the notes actually in the scale, it works well too. Since it is going down a half step and the scale actually covers that note.
Rudolpho: Now if the whole song is in the key of A minor, for example, when you do your riffs and stuff, do you stay within the key? Like do you use all diatonic notes like that?
Gil: For the most part, but…
Rudolpho: Or does it really matter when the chord changes?
Gil: See the thing with what I do, it doesn't really matter if I change with the chords, but it sounds better when I change with the chords…
Rudolpho: It seems like it fits more.
Gil: Right. Like if you make the chord significant, it is going to sound better. But if I don't change chords, if I just keep doing the scale, it won't sound messed up, you know what I mean? Yeah, but it obviously sounds better if the chords are made significant.
Rudolpho: Is that just a jazz thing?
Gil: Sort of, but jazz musicians have to change chords more or less, you know what I mean? It's like a middle school jazz thing [laughter].
Rudolpho: Right, right [laughing].

Within this reflective conversation on their playing, Gil and Rudolpho shared their knowledge about music theory and in doing so enriched each other's understanding of why they do what they do on their respective instruments. Rudolpho also deferred to Gil during the conversation, asking him why he was playing what he was playing, learning from Gil how to replicate it on the piano. Rudolpho recognized Gil's understanding of the fundamentals of jazz. He also praised Gil for the musical decisions that he made by commenting on what a nice sound it was.

Another kind of conversation occurred when Rudolpho professed that he was "trained so that everything needs to make sense." At this point, Gil became an authority on Steve Coleman and free jazz: "Go to Tower. Yeah, Tower will have it, and pick up *The Tao of Mad Phat*." Rudolpho repeated the title with a chuckle. Gil continued, "Yeah. You'll love it. The key signatures are ridiculous. We got to play it in high school, and it's ridiculous that we got to play it."

Rudolpho nodded and said, "Like C double sharp minor?"

Gil nodded back and said, "Yeah, like that stuff and [Steve Coleman] will be doing something crazy and then his guitar player will be playing some down-to-earth blues and in a different way it is just as crazy, you know? And there's bass lines played against the trumpet. The bass line will be in one key signature, and the trumpet will be in another key signature, and they meet up at the bridge."

Rudolpho interjected, "Polytonality."

"Yeah, it is crazy."

Rudolpho rubbed his forehead, groaned, and smiled. "Very crazy."

Gil then put his guitar down and said, "Here, let me play him" as he moved over to the keyboard. Rudolpho got out of the chair and gave Gil some room. Gil moved his hands up and down the keyboard and then asked Rudolpho, "Where are the drum patches?" Rudolpho pointed to the lower register of the keyboard. "Oh, OK. I want to just show you the Coleman beat." Gil found the sound of the drum that he wanted and then played the complicated 5/4 rhythm that begins the Steve Coleman piece.

Through conversations like this, occurring with members of his extended community of practice, Gil was able to link his turntablism with other forms of music and other musicians. He was able to see how the ways in which he manipulated records on turntables was similar to the improvisational style of jazz. At the same time, he imagined that the way in which he performed on his turntables would be similar to the way jazz artists perform:

> I think [turntablism's]...related to jazz because I'm going to just take all of the records that I am considering using, put them on the table, and grab them if I hear it. Like if I hear that there should be a siren next or a modem or someone's voice or someone rapping or someone singing then I'll just, you know, it's like improv. If you are using the blues scale in a solo and it gets boring and you switch to a pentatonic to give it some flavor or like a harmonic minor, you just hear that. Same thing.

These kinds of uncommon spaces—church, jazz band, and the recording studio—were actually integral to Gil's interest in and ability to develop his skills in turntablism. Gil performed, reflected, evaluated, and interpreted within these spaces for different reasons in relation to his turntablism. These spaces provided a general atmosphere of creative work that echoed and mirrored Gil's own passion for music. Seeking out these creative spaces, where youth like him were in the act of producing music, encouraged Gil to continue pursuing his own creative work. These spaces connected him to multiple communities of practice, communities that engaged in different kinds of musical expression. The jazz band was a community of practice that worked intensively to play jazz music; the church house band was a community of practice that learned gospel music; and Gil's connection with Rudolpho exposed him to the language and theory of classical music.

These spaces served as stages for essential discourses for Gil's work as a turntablist as well. These discourses provided content for Gil's turntablism and techniques for how to form a work habit. For example, Mr. Talbot stressed the hard work needed in order to play and perform. Through this hard work, he argued, players like Gil could risk experimenting on their instrument. Within the spaces of the church, jazz band, and the studio, Gil was made important through this language. The leader of the church house band praised Gil and the drummers for their skill on their respective instruments. She extended an invitation to Gil to play with the band for "many more days," acknowledging Gil's contribution. She also presented an imagined future of fame and fortune for the drummers. She imagined they would someday be on a world tour. While she may have been joking, this positive evaluation is significant and I think contributed to Gil wanting to continue developing his skills as a musician and turntablist. These spaces, along with Gil's work with Rudolpho, could remain disparate and unconnected without Gil reflecting on how they informed one another and contributed to his ability to excel in each.

Throughout this chapter, I illustrated how Gil utilized the six habits of mind and body within a variety of spaces to influence his creative practice. For example, through his experience in jazz band, Gil saw the similarity between improvising on the guitar and on his turntables. While hunting for records, Gil drew from disparate content in the form of musical genres—classical, children's music, jazz, soundtracks, country and western—in order to construct new music. I have done this in part to argue that creative practices are disparate, meaning that the process of constructing knowledge in practices like zine writing, turntablism, and graffiti is not linear or place-bound. In addition, school learning is often counterintuitive to the ways in which youth engage in meaning making in their lives.

Gil interpreted multiple sources in order to create music on his turntables. He also used his turntables as a way to place his personal life in context. I have shown a bit of that in the way in which I think Gil "agrees" with the song "E Pluribus Unum." One could argue, however, that Gil was not necessarily being a turntablist when he played that song. It is true that he did not manipulate the record in any way and he did not blend it with other records. Consequently, I would like to conclude this chapter by providing a glimpse into Gil's process of interpreting records and the ways in which he interpreted his own life through the music that he made.

GIL ON THE DECKS AT HOME: TURNTABLIST AS HISTORIAN

Gil did not practice only at school. His primary place to practice was in his room at home where he kept his equipment and records. When I would show up at Gil's house to watch him spin, he would greet me at the front door and ask if I wanted to see what he had been working on in terms of his turntables. We would then jog up the flight of stairs to his bedroom.

The first thing that inevitably grabbed my attention upon entering Gil's room was his enormous queen-size bed. It took up most of the room, with the wood headboard occupying the space between the two windows that looked onto the street. I often listened to Gil play while sitting on the edge of the wooden footboard of this bed until it became far too uncomfortable and I would end up sitting on the plush tan carpet.

Across from the footboard of his bed were Gil's turntables and mixer. They sat in his black coffin—the term used for the long, rectangular carrying case needed to lug around a turntablist's equipment—on top of his white chest of drawers. Gil said it was the perfect height for him. To the right of his turntables were his cardboard boxes of records: four in all. The records that he most often used when he spun stood stacked on their edges either directly to the left of his feet as he played or behind the mixer. To the left of his turntables was a wardrobe, on top of which sat his TV. Often the TV was on when he played. Around the room were objects that represented his other interests. I got the sense that his room was a collage of many years of life, and that some objects may have clashed with the way Gil thought of himself in the present. For example, there was the computer drawing of a human figure holding a guitar, resembling the symbol used to delineate the men's restroom from the women's. A pair of stilts leaned against a slim floor-to-ceiling bookshelf. Next to these stilts was his hockey stick. "I used to play when I was in sixth grade," Gil told me. His paintball gun hung over his bed, and an army helmet sat on one of the bookshelves.

Next to his bed hung a corkboard with one small article from *Jive* magazine thumb-tacked to the bottom:

DJs: Perhaps the easiest parallel one can draw between the South Bronx mixing OGs and their effect on future generations is the legacy of the 1940s and '50s blues legends on the rock guitar gods of the 1960s and '70s. Just as the instrumental and compositional creativity of modern rock predecessors like Chuck Berry, Bo Diddley, and Muddy Waters inspired the amplified fretwork frenetics of Jimi Hendrix, Eric Clapton, and Jimmy Page (subsequently causing kids worldwide to pick up guitars), so too did DJ Kool Herc, Afrika Bambaataa, Grand Wizard Theodore, and Grandmaster Flash inspire the first wave of post-old school pyro-techno-theatrical phenoms: DJs Scratch, Cash Money, Jazzy Jeff, and Aladdin.

On this particular day, Gil wanted to show me some work he had been doing with two albums of speeches by Martin Luther King Jr. and Malcolm X. A friend from school had loaned him the albums a few days before. He placed each album on the turntables, turned on the mixer, placed the headphones over his ears, and dropped the right turntable needle on the revolving record. Malcolm X's voice boomed out of the speaker:

…are waking up and they are gaining a new political consciousness, becoming politically mature, and as they develop this political maturity, they are able to see the recent trends in these political elections. They see that whites are so evenly divided that every time they vote, the racist polls have to go back and count the votes all over again.…In fact I think we would be fooling ourselves if we had an audience this large and didn't realize that there were some enemies in it.

Gil started scratching the phrase "in it" from the Malcolm X speech and then allowed it to continue playing: *This afternoon we want to talk about the ballot or the bullet.* Gil then sampled and scratched "bullet" over and over again. At this point in his playing, I asked Gil what interested him about these two albums: "Well, like, it relates to today. I'll show you specifically with me and [my school] how it relates."

The turntable with Malcolm X continued to spin; however, by moving the cross-fader of the mixer over to the left, no sound came out of the speaker. Gil then placed the Martin Luther King album on the left turntable. He placed the needle on the album, flicked the cross-fader to the right again, and Malcolm X's voice bellowed, "Well, this country is a hypocrite. They try to make you think they set you free by calling you a second-class citizen. No, you nothing but a 20th-century slave." Gil flicked the cross-fader to the left, and Martin Luther King spoke: "This nation is wrong because it is nothing but a new form of slavery."

Gil started juggling the phrases "You nothing but a 20th-century slave" from Malcolm X and "This nation is wrong" from Martin Luther King Jr. By juggling, I mean that he went back and forth between these two phrases, sometimes allowing the whole phrase to play before he spliced the other in, sometimes only playing bits and pieces of each. Sometimes, he played both at the same time, so that the voices overlapped with one another. I asked him why he made the choice to juggle these two phrases:

> The contrast between what they are saying and the similarities… They are talking about two different things. [Malcolm X] is talking about colonization with the second-class citizenship. And [Martin Luther King Jr.] is talking about segregation and they are sort of the same thing but they are kind of different names for it. They kind of look at it from a different point of view…Segregation is sort of a name that is sort of geared toward the 1960s and the Civil Rights Movement. And second-class citizenship and colonization sort of like general and sort of like looking at history in general…so they are both saying that it is basically slavery. [Malcolm X] is saying the new form of slavery or 20th-century slavery and [Martin Luther King Jr.] is saying new form of slavery.

By playing these two speeches simultaneously, Gil interprets the subtle differences in the ways Malcolm X and Martin Luther King Jr. discuss oppression. Gil is able to hear how Malcolm X utilizes references to history and Martin Luther King Jr. utilizes more contemporary representations of oppression. The act of sampling from these speeches for Gil was not simply indiscriminately dropping the needle. Part of his work involved hours of listening to the albums until he knew them inside and out. Therefore, on the day he showed me this work, he constructed a spontaneous message out of bits of text he knew by heart, much like the improvisational playing of a jazz guitarist. Gil never "performed" this piece. In other words, he did not play it for a larger audience other than me. However, this space served as more than a time to hone his technical skills as a turntablist. Through this space and time, Gil manipulated historical sources in order to construct his own meaning. In this case, he used his turntables to interpret a historic event—the Civil Rights Movement—as well as the different connotations of the term "slavery" from the perspective of two of the movement's leaders. Through playing these voices on his turntables, remixing them the way that he did, he was able to hear the rhetorical differences in the way Malcolm X and Martin Luther King Jr. understood the current climate of racial injustice in the 1960s.

It is useful to compare Gil's work to the kind of research that many teachers expect of their students. In this case, the two ways of making meaning are surprisingly similar. Gil worked and learned the way we wish all of our students would when they research. He first went graverobbing and spent hours at various new and used record stores and yard sales, as well as trading albums with friends and fellow turntablists. Then Gil spent several more hours over a period of days, listening to these albums, first all of the way through to get "the message," and then in bits and pieces, experimenting with particular scratches and phrases; Gil interpreted the vinyl texts. A part of understanding the messages of the albums also entailed reflective conversations with Sam. He would document these conversations in a notebook he carried in his pocket. This notebook also contained ideas for turntable pieces, lists of records he wanted to obtain, and names and contact information of people associated with turntablism. After finding the phrases he liked, he would begin putting the new text together. In order to construct this new interpretation, Gil cited from other people's work. Citing, in this case, is the phrases that he sampled from the records. This whole practice created a way for Gil to make what he "read" personally meaningful to him. He fashioned his own point.

After Gil played his piece, he told me that he had read the Malcolm X speech that he was manipulating in his English class that semester. But the act of reading the speech did not interest him nearly as much as playing it on his turntables:

> I think the idea of having a voice played of someone who's dead is really cool...Because it kind of brings them back to life, and not many things have that power. I actually feel that he is talking. I feel that he is alive when I hear the voice. We read the script of the speech in Lit class, the one where he's like, "I would be mistaken if we had a turnout this big and there weren't some enemies in here." And it was really cool to read that, but I felt like I was reading the speech of a dead guy...but when I play it on a record, it's almost like he's not here but he's over there [pointing to the corner of his room].

Through his turntables, the words of Malcolm X and Martin Luther King Jr. were no longer disembodied or "embalmed speech" to use Denzin's (1997) term. Rather, Gil had the power to resurrect their voices *and* interpret their messages in the life he lived. In the quote above, and through his work process, Gil speaks to a critical characteristic of an effective teacher: the ability to work with youth to find ways to make the texts with which they interact feel like they are "not here, but…[right] over there" within arm's reach, malleable, and connected to youth's lives in relevant ways.

CONCLUSION

The amount of time and effort that Gil devotes to his creative practice is considerable. The interesting thing to me is that it is not only the subject that stimulates Gil to work long hours on his creative practice but it is also the way in which he gets to work, the *craft* of his creative practice, that makes him stay up all hours on the turntables. In fact, the physicality of the work, and the freedom he has in determining when he wants to do it, influences the meanings that Gil makes in and through it. In the final chapter of this book, I offer ways for teachers to develop complex understandings of how youth like Gil, Miguel, and Ian work and learn on their own terms as a means to move beyond artificially constructed learning environments and into curricula and classrooms that take advantage of the skill and sophistication that students like Gil bring to school.

4

TEACHING AND LEARNING
A Shared Practice

Youth like Gil, Miguel, and Ian have rich learning lives that run parallel to and intersect with their school learning lives. How can we, as teachers, design learning environments that embody habits that youth feel are personally relevant, useful, and meaningful? How can we take advantage of the skills and conceptual knowledge that youth bring with them to school? Instead of viewing youth as empty vessels needing to be filled or as being deficient in some way, we need to see youth as complex people with valuable life and work experiences. One reason why we must view youth in this positive and constructive way is because of the alarming trends in public education, particularly at the middle and high school levels.

For example, according to a recent study conducted by Civic Enterprises (Bridgeland, DeIulio, & Morison, 2006) for the Bill and Melinda Gates Foundation, one third of high school students do not graduate on time. Within African American, Hispanic, and Native American populations, 50% do not graduate within 4 years. Among these students, 90% had passing grades when they dropped out. A primary reason students give for dropping out is that they found classes to be boring. In the report, the authors recommended that one way to address what they call the "silent epidemic" is to design curriculum that is more personally meaningful for students.

It is commonly understood that 30% of teachers leave the profession within the first 5 years of their careers. A recent study conducted by the National Center for Education Statistics shows that 38% of all teachers who leave teaching claim that lack of support from administration played a significant role in their decision to leave. Thirty-two percent left because of dissatisfaction with school conditions. Both these reasons can be addressed in part through a redefining of what it means to be a teacher and a student in the classroom.

With these understandings of how Miguel, Ian, and Gil work on their own terms, we can now imagine how their habits of performance, experimentation, evaluation, reflection, and interpretation can inform the way teachers design learning environments. In order to do that, I first discuss how Dewey and contemporary scholars push us to take seriously the skills and knowledge that youth bring with them to school as a way of showing that there is a precedent for teaching through the creative capacities of youth. I also make the case that the current trend of hyper-standardized curriculum actually gets in the way of creating the next generation of mathematicians, historians, scientists, and writers.

Next, I discuss my experience with how teachers, new and veteran, often limit youth creative practices to products that they can bring into the classroom rather than seeing the everyday practices as ways of informing work done *in* the classroom. I suggest that in order for classrooms to truly honor the way youth work on their own terms, we need to move beyond thinking of their work as products and instead understand them as habits of mind and body that youth develop and employ in order to create personally meaningful learning experiences. This orientation to teaching moves teachers and students from being interpreters of knowledge to being appropriators of learning practices. I advocate that teachers view themselves as ethnographers and amateurs. Teachers who see themselves like this are able to imagine how multiple forms of performance, reflection, evaluation, experimentation, and communities of practice can be habits of mind and body that drive the learning of their own classrooms.

The last section of this chapter makes the case for how the theory and practice of inquiry-based learning provides an infrastructure that both enables the teacher to be an ethnographer and amateur and supports how youth learn on their own terms. Specifically, I discuss the idea of designing a curriculum as infrastructure as opposed to structure. Curriculum as infrastructure provides a space for youth to engage in personally meaningful work that feels and sounds like Aristotle's "intrinsic aesthetic or crafting that underlies the practices of everyday life." Through designing learning experiences that build on the intrinsic work habits of youth, we can in part address the current criticisms many students and teachers have about middle schools and high schools.

BELIEVING IN YOUTH AS CREATIVE AND
INTELLIGENT HUMAN BEINGS

The idea of valuing the knowledge and experience that youth bring with them to school is not new. In fact, Dewey argued for this stance on teaching and learning when he wrote, "What we need is something which will enable us to interpret, to appraise, the elements in the child's present puttings forth and fallings away, his exhibitions of power and weakness, in the light of some larger growth-process in which they have their place" (Dewey, 1966, p. 14). The "present puttings forth" in this case are the skills and knowledge that children or youth bring from their collective experience to school. The "place" that Dewey refers to means finding ways to blend the *life learning* of children with the goals and objectives of *school learning*.

Contemporary scholars like Ayers, Wiggins, and Starnes and Paris advocate for this stance as well. Ayers (1998) writes that teachers need to "see each student as a three-dimensional creature with hopes, dreams, aspirations, skills, and capacities; with body, mind, heart, and spirit; with experience, history, and future" (p. 53). Wiggins makes the case for designing school learning environments around the habits of mind and body of youth like Gil, Miguel, and Ian when he writes, "Only by apprenticing in the hands-on work of knowledge production can students learn to turn inchoate feeling and received opinions into unforgettable, vibrant, and systematized knowledge" (1989, p. 45). Starnes and Paris contend that a rigorous school learning environment "involves learners in making significant decisions about how they will learn, how they will assess what they learn, and how they will use what they have learned in meaningful ways" (2000, p. 2). Gil, Miguel, and Ian embody these three characteristics of "academic integrity" as Starnes and Paris describe it in the ways in which they approach their creative practices.

These educational philosophers and others call for the catalyst for pedagogical change to be the learning experience of youth outside of schools. This orientation fits loosely within "constructivism"—the belief that students construct their own understandings of the world. A constructivist pedagogy is becoming a rare practice within classrooms, particularly with the emphasis on standardized testing and a micro-managed curriculum. When it is practiced, often the understanding being constructed begins *in* the classroom. The habits of mind and body originate and are developed within that space as opposed to the lives of the youth. Often teachers feel that they need to "find" what it is that they need to learn *in* the classroom rather than beginning by understanding the skills and concepts that youth already possess and building from there. Rarer still is the discussion of youth work as *practice* as opposed to *product* followed by concrete ways of embodying the practice into classrooms.

Unfortunately, the current catalyst for pedagogical change, more often than not, comes from bureaucrats or small interest groups whose least concern is how youth develop sustainable learning environments in their lives. Ironically, it is not their concern how youth develop into historians, scientists, mathematicians, or writers. What is more, impetus for pedagogical change tends to come from a need adults feel for youth to be more proficient in some kind of skill in order for the United States to be more competitive in the world economy. For example, No Child Left Behind mandates that children must be able to independently read by the third grade but not because of any real-world need felt within the child. It is because educational bureaucrats within the federal government have legislated it as being essential so that they can better (read "more easily") monitor and evaluate the "quality" of the education a child has within a public school (see Callahan, 1962).

Shultz and Cook-Sather suggests that teachers and administrators do not allow youth ways of working and learning to influence pedagogy because of a lack of trust they have for youth to make sound decisions and judgments. This lack of trust results in students being "dehumanized, reduced to products, and most certainly devoid of those qualities that would make them authorities" (Shultz & Cook-Sather, 2001, p. 3). Continuing with this theme of distrust, districts and schools do not trust teachers to make wise choices, which further stifles creativity and diversity with respect to how teachers teach and how students learn (Meier, 2002).

To push this idea of the disjuncture between youth ways of knowing and schooling a bit further, Dewey observed that the curriculum most often is designed for the adult mind rather than for the child's mind. He wrote, "The studies as classified are the product, in a word, of the science of the ages, not of the experience of the child" (Dewey, 1966, p. 7). Dewey argued that when curriculum is designed for the adult mind, it creates unnecessary learning obstacles for the child or the youth because they do not approach problems, issues, ideas, or concepts in the same ways as adults: "The source of whatever is dead, mechanical, and formal in schools is found precisely in the subordination of the life and experience of the child to the curriculum. It is because of this that 'study' has become a synonym for what is irksome, and a lesson identical to a task" (p. 9). An adult mind, Dewey argued, can do the logical ordering of meaning after experience. Youth cannot do that kind of adult learning behavior if they have not engaged in actually experiencing what it is that they are trying to learn. Too often, adults kill the potential for active learning by trying to order the knowledge in some artificial way or by simply removing experience from the learning altogether. Through seeing Gil, Miguel, and Ian work in their everyday lives, we see how knowledge that they construct comes out of a deep immersion into multiple experiences within their creative practices. This is how youth learn, and Dewey argues that we should fashion curriculum and pedagogy around this way of being as opposed to the detached adult way of teaching that dominates schools.

MOVING FROM INTERPRETATION TO APPROPRIATION: YOUTH CULTURE AS LEGITIMATE WORK AND LEARNING

Lave and Wenger (1991) write, "There is a difference between talking *about* a practice from outside and talking *within* it" (p. 107). Their argument is a distillation of the distinction between interpretation and appropriation. Teaching and learning as interpretation talk *about* a practice. When students learn about poetry in schools, for example, they often talk about what a poem means. Teaching and learning as appropriation talk *within* the practice. From this pedagogical perspective, students would discuss poetry while writing in the form themselves. Teachers often fit youth culture in their classrooms through designing units of study around the products of the practice: graffiti, rap, zines, etc. Teachers design classes around interpreting youth culture products, gleaning meaning from studying them rather than appropriating the habits of mind and body that make the work happen.

Teachers who see youth culture as potential units of study are informed about popular culture more broadly. They value this popular culture as high art and potentially part of the "canon." These teachers help their students see that they can view anything as a source of learning. Placing popular culture at the center of the curriculum legitimates it and allows students to speak about their own experiences within the classroom. Nevertheless, youth do not necessarily want their cultural practices to be legitimated or co-opted by teachers or schools. In fact, adult sanctions of popular culture may ironically delegitimate it as an interesting world of experience; it may be the exact opposite of what youth "want." I am reminded of Moje's (2002) finding that youth with whom she works often "dismiss" texts that progressive educators think are relevant. Youth might "see through this" as trying to trick them into learning; that is, they may very well interpret a teacher's genuine interest in the art form as an attempt to motivate them to participate. If the teacher's interest in the art form is merely a tool of motivation or interpretation, students will read this as an ultimate dismissal of their interests, rather than as a "cool" way to learn. Also, not everyone is "into" graffiti like Miguel, for example. If teachers head down this road, they could set up all sorts of obstacles for certain students to get involved with whatever it is that they are exploring in the classroom. Finally, making something a subject of study can "fix it" in such a way that it loses its vitality. In the same way that a Shakespearean play can be boring to read, graffiti could be boring if it is something studied rather than something *lived*.

Certainly, challenging privileged ways of knowledge through interpreting "counterliteracy" forms must be a part of reconceptualizing how we work and learn in classrooms. It serves to break down the barrier between in-school and out-of-school knowledge and acknowledges the interests of youth. As we saw in the previous chapters, what Gil, Miguel, and Ian produce are important to them: turntable pieces, zines, graffiti, and tattoos. Interpreting existing cultural forms is a part of that work too: recall Gil's interpretation of the two speeches by Malcolm X and Martin Luther King Jr. that he blended together while practicing one day or the way in which Miguel moved to canvas after he viewed a gallery opening of contemporary graffiti artists. That said, we need to move beyond product-based forms of pedagogy to a more process-based orientation. We need to appropriate the practices that make it possible for the products to be produced. The goal is not to turn all of our students into graffiti artists or turntablists or zine writers. Rather, we need to look underneath the products of these art forms to the common rituals, routines, and skills that youth within these and other practices employ in order to do the work. With this process-based understanding of youth work, we can then reorient the work in classrooms to appropriate these youth ways of learning.

Most of Gil, Miguel, and Ian's time spent in their creative practices involved performance, experimentation, communities of practice, evaluation, reflection, and interpretation. These aspects of their creative practices *must* exist in order for any kind of product to be made. I have found that it can be difficult for teachers to switch from a product- or interpretation-based pedagogy to a process- or appropriation-based pedagogy. In other words, it is fairly easy to see how rap songs, for example, can be added to the list of literature that can be interpreted in class. However, this product-based way of understanding how youth make meaning in their lives does not necessarily change the way work is *done* in the classroom.

We have a better chance of changing the work culture of classrooms if we focus our attention on the craft of youth work. When we consider youth and the work they do as an everyday practice, a nice parallel can be drawn with teachers and the work that they do in their classrooms. In the case of this book, Gil, Ian, and Miguel make cultural products in their lives (zines and spoken word pieces, turntable compositions, and graffiti pieces and tattoos). Teachers make something in their classrooms. They are in the act of designing classroom environments that stimulate and challenge students to develop skills and conceptual knowledge. When we understand youth work as practice and teaching as practice, ways into seeing how the former can influence the latter become apparent.

Wenger writes, "What we think about learning influences where we recognize learning, as well as what we do when we decide that we must do something about it—as individuals, as communities, and as organizations" (1998, p. 9). The ways in which Gil, Ian, and Miguel learn and work on their own terms pushes us to ask the question: How can the ways in which these youth work in their creative practices—the "intrinsic aesthetic or crafting that underlies the practices"—influence the daily activity, the ways of working, in classrooms? I see teachers addressing this question in two interconnected ways: as ethnographers and amateurs in their classrooms *and* then as conscious designers of the learning experience.

BECOMING ETHNOGRAPHERS AND AMATEURS

One way to get at answers to the question above is through developing an ethnographic understanding of how youth make meaning in their own lives (Goswami & Stillman, 1987; Lytle, 2001; Schultz, 2003; Sitton, 1980). Ethnography focuses on the daily lives of sets of people who associate regularly together (in local networks, institutions, or communities) and on what their everyday experience means to them. Ethnographers observe, interview, and participate in the routine activities of the people they study. But the interest is not in local phenomena alone. Rather it is in connections between locally situated activity and broader realms of symbolic meaning and social organization. Modern ethnography also searches beyond the local setting for more general demographic and historical information, considering how and to what extent local people's actions both influence and are influenced by wider social arenas and social forces. Ethnography makes visible the ordinary and taken-for-granted details of what particular people do together. It is sensitive to nuances. It identifies cultural frames for acting and making sense that vary and change as individuals and groups occupy differing positions in society. Special attention is paid by ethnographers to the situations of race, gender, ethnicity, language group, and social class in the organization of social life.

Ethnographers approach their phenomena realizing that they know little and that the people who are part of the phenomena, the "natives," know a lot. With this realization, ethnographers position themselves as the learners and the people who are part of the phenomena as the teachers. They *observe, interview, and participate* in order to better understand the people whom they are studying. When we make this analogous to teaching, it is our job as teachers to figure out how our students are mathematicians, historians, writers, and scientists *in their lives*, instead of assuming that they are not or that they need to be taught how to be. Teacher-ethnographers collect bits of youth conversation, notes thrown out in the trash, and other kinds of artifacts. They recognize dress, musical tastes, and cultural movements. Teacher-ethnographers use these data to not only inform them in terms of who the youth are as people but to also inform their understanding of how the ways youth work and learn in their worlds are ways into being mathematicians, historians, scientists, and writers. Therefore, a teacher who is influenced by ethnographic practices would no longer look at Ian's interest in zine writing as simply a product. Instead, the teacher would recognize that Ian is involved in a practice—habits of mind and body—that enables him to do the work of a writer.

From a curriculum standpoint we would call this lifework that Ian is engaged in "experience." Dewey writes:

> Experience does not go on simply inside a person. It does go on there, for it influences the formation of attitudes of desire and purpose. But this is not the whole of the story. Every genuine experience has an active side which changes in some degree the objective conditions under which experiences are had…
>
> …We live from birth to death in a world of persons and things which in large measure is what it is because of what has been done and transmitted from previous human activities. When this fact is ignored, experience is treated as if it were something which goes on exclusively inside an individual's body and mind.…There are sources outside an individual which give rise to experience. It is constantly fed from these springs.…Ordinarily we take such facts for granted as too commonplace to record. But when their educational import is recognized, they indicate [a] way in which the educator can direct the experience of the young without engaging in imposition. (Dewey, 1997, pp. 39–40)

Dewey argues that one's learning life is influenced by both outside and inside forces. He refers to these outside forces as "persons and things." The persons and things that youth interact with are in part influenced by what the youth have experienced in their pasts. These past people and things influence present people and things, which shape future experiences. Instead of taking this truism for granted, as Dewey suggests many people do, he pushes us to look into the "human activities" of youth for their "educational import." In other words, the everyday experiences of youth are sophisticated, meaningful, and not unlike the knowledge teachers expect students to develop in schools. The "educational import" of the creative practices of Miguel, Ian, and Gil lay in their use of performance and experimentation; their development of communities of practice; and their practice of evaluation, reflection, and interpretation. Dewey suggests that if we tune our teaching practice to these habits, we will avoid the pitfall of imposing learning on students. This imposition has many deleterious results. On the one hand, students may eventually drop out because of sheer boredom. On the other, those who choose to stay will develop learning habits that do not prepare them to be mathematicians, historians, writers, and scientists.

The teacher-ethnographer realizes that it is part of his or her job to understand the how and why of the practice because it is one of the ways in which youth make meaning. A teacher who takes an ethnographic stance finds ways to understand the depth and complexity of Gil's turntablism, for example. She works to see how Gil is reflective, experimental, and evaluative in the way that he works on his own terms. A teacher-ethnographer thinks, "How can I utilize these ways of being in my math class so that Gil can work as a mathematician?" She comes to know the community of practice Miguel keeps in order to be able to do his work. She honors that sophistication through the way in which she teaches.

Understanding youth cultural practices as an ethnographer requires that we look at youth as inherently creative problem posers and problem solvers. The teacher enters his room assuming that his students are already some form of mathematician, scientist, poet, architect, etc. Gallas writes that she "suspend[s] [her] disbelief as a teacher and [leaves her] judgment in abeyance in service of a child's development" (1994, p. 96). She continues: "Rather than my 'teaching'…what science [is], we [struggle] together to understand [our] changing picture of science" (p. 96).

Edward Said would describe Gallas as an "amateur," someone who doesn't limit herself through special knowledge of a discipline. Experts, Said contrasts, only feel comfortable approaching problems, issues, or ideas through their rarified knowledge. He warns that specialization, as opposed to competence, can result in the "sacrifice of one's general culture to a set of authorities and canonical ideas" (1996, p. 76). He adds:

> Specialization means losing sight of the raw effort of constructing either art or knowledge; as a result you cannot view knowledge and art as choices and decisions, commitments and alignments, but only in terms of impersonal theories or methodologies....In the end...you become tame and accepting of whatever the so-called leaders in the field will allow. Specialization also kills your sense of excitement and discovery...giving up to specialization is, I have always felt, laziness, so you end up doing what others tell you, because that is your specialty after all. (p. 77)

When someone presents an expert with a problem that grows out of her creative practice, an expert often feels that she cannot even discuss it because it is beyond the purview of her expertise. What she knows has nothing to do with the problem. Teachers often think of themselves or approach their subject as experts or specialists. For example, a math teacher may see his job as teaching students how to factor polynomials and therefore cannot afford the time to link the practice of mathematics with the habits of mind and body of turntablists or graffiti writers or even be able to entertain a provocative tangent related to everyday life. Said suggests that teachers who view themselves as specialists are not able to see the "raw effort" of work and learning. They are blind to the practices—the daily habits of mind and body—that lead to the construction of knowledge. Instead, they focus on the end result: the knowledge itself. This blindness may also lead to a lack of genuine interest or "excitement," to use Said's term, regarding understanding the world around us. Specialization makes it difficult for teachers to believe that youth are mathematicians, for example, because they do not have the rarified knowledge that the teacher has. It also makes it incredibly easy to view one's job as teacher as "doing what others tell you" instead of as a creative enterprise fraught with "choices...decisions, commitments, and alignments."

Teachers who view themselves as amateurs, on the other hand, pounce on these opportunities to think about things differently and learn from others. Said defines amateurism as "an activity that is fueled by care and affection rather than by profit and selfish, narrow specialization" (p. 82). Teachers can see their students as allies in a common project. They expect to learn from their students, not just how to be better teachers or how to understand fractions in a new way but also about the world in general. Said writes that teachers as amateurs "can enter and transform the merely professional routine most of us go through into something much more lively and radical; instead of doing what one is supposed to do one can ask why one does it, who benefits from it, how can it reconnect with a personal project and original thoughts" (p. 83). Teachers who see themselves as amateurs value students' experiences in creative practices as resources for their own understandings of academic subject knowledge in particular and the world more broadly.

Gil, Miguel, and Ian, like so many youth, are amateurs as well. What makes them amateurs are the range and variety of things that they do that somehow influence how they make their particular art forms. For example, Gil reads widely. He plays guitar in his church band. He raps, break dances, and views films. He writes music and listens to music. Gil redesigns his car. He does not pursue these experiences solely because of his interest in turntablism. Nevertheless, they inform and influence what and how he decides to work on his turntables. These disparate sources are "outside an individual which give rise to" the way in which Gil interacts with his turntables. Like Gallas, teachers who understand youth work as craft provide spaces where students can see for themselves that the skills and concepts that they are developing within their creative practices are assets in the classroom. All of Gil's varied experiences can be used in the classroom to do the work of the class. Students as amateurs see their craft as informing and influencing the way they engage in the work of the class. They see academic disciplines and their creative practices as equal resources for their work.

This example is an interesting confluence of many sources. At the time, Gil was studying the Civil Rights Movement in school. He had read many of the famous speeches of that era. He also had tacit knowledge of racism and oppression through his personal experience as an African American as well as through the politically charged music that he listened to. A friend loaned Gil two albums of Martin Luther King Jr. and Malcolm X speeches. His turntables were a vehicle through which Gil could reinterpret these texts. Gil recognized the value of his course work and deepened the meaning and significance of that work through bringing together these disparate "persons and things." I hazard a guess that studying the Civil Rights Movement would not have been nearly as interesting for Gil had he not employed the habits of mind and body inherent in his work as a turntablist.

Teachers who do not see themselves as amateurs often get stuck in the infinite loop of trying to *find* something to do with their students. Teaching becomes a constant search for the best activities to fill an hour, day, or week because teaching as an expert often views knowledge as bits of information to be digested. Lave (1997) captures this perpetual crisis of teaching by comparing a curriculum that supports the creative practices of youth with a curriculum that delineates what that practice must be:

> The problem is that any curriculum intended to be a specification *of* practice, rather than an arrangement of opportunities *for* practice (for fashioning and resolving ownable dilemmas) is bound to result in the teaching of a misanalysis of practice…and the learning of still another. At best it can only induce a new and exotic kind of practice.…In the settings for which it is intended (in everyday transactions), it will appear out of order and will not in fact reproduce "good" practice. (p. 32)

Lave cautions us that the focus in classrooms should not be *on* practice or the interpretation of practice, meaning an emphasis on learning facts and procedural skills outside the context of the practice itself. Instead, teachers should spend their pedagogical energy on designing experiences where students can appropriate a practice. In this case, Lave calls these experiences "ownable dilemmas." These are challenges, problems, or obstacles that students want to take on, see the purpose in solving, and feel the need to overcome. A curriculum where youth utilize skills and conceptual knowledge developed through creative practices is designed around "ownable dilemmas" for that is exactly the way in which youth engage in their work on their own terms. Their daily practice places them in perplexing, confusing, or challenging moments where they must do more work in order to move forward in their art form. Lave also suggests that when we place students in the role of interpreters of a discipline, rather than as practitioners within a discipline, "a new and exotic kind of practice" results. In other words, students as interpreters of a discipline are not learning what it is to be a mathematician, scientist, historian, and writer. They are learning a misinterpretation of what it means to be any of these kinds of professionals.

A youth orientation to work and learning is more sustainable than the kind of curriculum that is built from daily lessons and one-off activities. Instead, teachers design learning environments that encourage a way of being in the classroom, as opposed to a collection of methods of teaching. Implementing this sort of curriculum gives teachers a "solution" to the problem of constantly trying to find one day, one month, or one hour of something to do in the classroom. Lemke reminds us that "practices are not just performances, not just behaviors, not just material processes or operations, but meaningful actions, actions that have relations of meaning to one another in terms of some cultural system" (1997, p. 43). There is value in building a "common culture" of amateurs in our classrooms in order to enable our students to "learn not just what and how to perform, but also what the performance means" (p. 43). It is in this spirit that we can build with our students a "community of classroom practice" through the conception of creative practice—youth work—as craft.

DESIGNING THE LEARNING EXPERIENCE

Once a teacher sees his role as, in part, developing a sense of the culture of work of his students, he can then do the work of translating that understanding into how he designs the learning experience. The ethnographic/amateur stance informs how one goes about designing a learning experience. The teacher can open up space in the classroom for youth like Gil, Miguel, and Ian to utilize the technical skills and conceptual knowledge acquired through their creative practices. I do not mean that students like Gil, Miguel, and Ian should engage in turntablism, graffiti, and zine writing in the class. Rather, I mean that these students should be encouraged to use the habits of mind and body that are a part of these crafts to do the work of the class. They should intuit that their ways of learning on their own terms are valued and necessary. What I would like to do now is take the aspects of Miguel's, Gil's, and Ian's practices that I have been exploring in this book and translate them into classroom practice. Specifically, I will discuss how teachers can implement various forms of performance, experimentation, communities of practice, evaluation, reflection, and interpretation into their classroom design as ways of creating classroom spaces that allow youth to work and learn on their own terms.

Multiple Forms of Performance and Experimentation

Performance often has a narrow definition in classrooms. In a classroom context, performance often means displaying some kind of product at the end of a unit. Performance is used as a sign of the end of learning a concept or set of skills: the culmination of several weeks of work. It could be a "public" reading involving students sharing their writing in front of the rest of the class. A performance could be a museum of artifacts produced through research students did in a history class. The performance is polished and practiced. It is meant to be one's best effort. The performance is also a way for teachers to grade the work of their students. When the performance concludes, the class moves on to something else, and this something else is tied to curricular objectives that are often not connected at all to the learning that led up to that performance.

The multidimensional uses of performance described in this book push us to expand the way in which we design performances in our classrooms. Many times, Gil, Miguel, or Ian developed a particular product out of snippets of ideas amassed over a period of time. In fact, these youth would purposefully perform works in progress designed in this way to push their creative practices forward. An example is Ian's second reading at the Painted Bride where he determined that he probably should not have read his piece but through the process gained a deeper understanding of his writing voice and the purpose behind the poem, or when Gil layered the Malcolm X and Martin Luther King Jr. speeches. Gil wanted to perform for me what he had been working on, not as a final product, but as a work in progress that, through performing, he could think about more critically. He performed this work in progress to open a space where we could talk about the issues introduced by the material. Miguel's graffiti drawings for family members communicated love and respect for them. His model building added to the décor of his room. Airbrushing his Timberland boots helped define who he was. The tattooing could be considered an embodied performance. All of these performances happened in the midst of his craft, not just at the end.

Besides end of unit culminations, we need to offer more informal forms of performance where our students can try their work out, in mid-production, like Gil, Miguel, and Ian so often do with their creative work. These informal performances serve a crucial purpose: They provide essential feedback from peers in order to determine where to go next or even if it is worth proceeding with the project at all. They also open up avenues for critical conversation about the craft itself and the meaning of the products being constructed. These performances provide opportunities for discussing the ideas within the work. Freedom must be given to students to decide, after such performances, whether they should abandon works and move on to other ideas that they are pursuing. I would also argue that multiple forms of performance create authentic reasons for students to experiment further, reflect on their work, evaluate its efficacy, and interpret audience reactions.

An important aspect of performance is experimentation. All three youth test out ideas within their creative practices to open up new possibilities in their work, to see what they were capable of, and to see what could be done under the circumstances. Gil spun new records in the music room to see what he could do with them. Ian improvised during Model United Nations as a way to stretch his writing voice. Miguel experimented with multiple art forms to find the one that he could sustain. They were attempts on Miguel's part to see what he could do within the real constraints of his life. Sometimes this experimentation was coupled with performance. Other times the experimentation occurred when the youth were alone practicing their craft. The important thing to remember here is that the three youth in this book, and I would argue anyone who is involved in a creative endeavor, employ experimentation to in some way reflect on or evaluate their craft as well as learn through their craft.

How can we as teachers implement experimentation and various forms of performance into our classroom designs? Imagine you are teaching a unit on short stories. You decide to have your students write their own short stories. Informed and influenced by the creative practices of the students in your class, specifically their use of multiple forms of performance and experimentation, you would not only have a culminating performance at the end of the unit where students would pick their "best" short story to read aloud or display. You would implement daily and weekly performances, informal readings, for example, where your students could try out stories as works in progress to see where to take them next or whether to drop them entirely for another idea. After all, isn't this reflection and evaluation what writers do? They work on getting ideas down on paper and then share those rough ideas with others whom they trust. This is different from sharing a rough draft of a piece that needs polishing. Youth and adults involved in a creative practice see feedback throughout the process of developing an idea. This feedback occurs through performing writing in midproduction.

Gil, Ian, and Miguel also performed widely. Gil performed in the music room, in his own room, in a studio, in a record store, in his friend's house, and at parties. Ian performed at open mics and through publishing his zines. He also played in a band as a vehicle for performing creative work. Miguel performed every day with the tattoo on his hand. He also performed through the graffiti pieces he made for his family and through wearing the boots that he airbrushed. If we want to design learning environments where the learning has the potential to be personally meaningful and resonate with how youth learn in the world, we must provide our students the chance to perform in small and large ways outside of the confines of our classrooms or schools. This pedagogical move creates the possibility of our students identifying multiple audiences for their work. These different audiences can push our students' work in new directions. For example, if students investigate how to improve the safety of a local intersection in your math class, they should not only perform their findings to a high level official in city government but they should also meet with urban planners, transportation advocates, and pedestrian advocates. At this time, students perform what they are learning not just to show what they know but also as a way of figuring out what needs to happen next.

Not surprisingly, experimentation as a learning practice is one of the first things to go in a standardized curriculum. Opportunities to invent or perform ideas on-the-fly are almost nonexistent when learning outcomes are predetermined. Experimentation is inherently open ended. The outcomes are surprising and oftentimes unintended. Time and time again, Miguel, Ian, and Gil showed me that experimentation was an essential aspect of their practice. Without it, they would not have been able to create what they did. With this understanding of experimentation as a part of authentic learning, time and space must be made available for students to think and act offhandedly. We need to give them situations, problems, and obstacles that are perplexing and demand invention and play. One way to do this in a chemistry or biology class is to have students design their own experiments, which do not have predetermined outcomes. In this kind of learning environment, students would come up with their own questions and devise experiments to answer them. All disciplines can implement warm-up activities where students are presented with a perplexing situation that they need to think and act their way out of. The key here is that the answers are not predetermined. In other words, a math problem that has a definable answer does not meet the criteria for this kind of experimental work. The answer is not what is important. It is the way in which one thinks and acts within the question or situation that creates the opportunity for developing new understandings and apprenticing as a scientist or mathematician, for example.

Embracing Idiosyncratic Ways of Working

The youth in this study have peculiar and individual ways of making work meaningful to them. When you spend time with youth you find that they have their own personal ways of understanding the world about them and doing work in order to construct that understanding. These processes are certainly not axiomatic or linear. They also often do not mirror the ways in which an adult would learn in that particular circumstance. In their everyday lives, youth do not follow the regimented work patterns of classrooms: one day to brainstorm ideas, another day to read and take notes, another day to write a rough draft, etc. Instead, Gil, Miguel, and Ian, like other youth involved in these kinds of practices, work in fits and starts, sometimes dabbling, other times working for many hours at a stretch. While at work, they experiment. They test out ideas by themselves and with members of their community of practice. They hone particular technical skills.

For example, Gil told me that there would be days where he would come home from school and immediately get on his turntables. The next thing he knew he would look up at the clock and realize that he had been on them for six straight hours. By the end of the session, records would be strewn about the floor: evidence of intense work. Gil even rigged a cross-fader so that he could take it to bed with him and practice crabbing, a technique for moving the toggle switch of the cross-fader to create various effects as the record plays.

Miguel had to take advantage of any time and space in order to do his work. He told me on many occasions that he would wait until late at night in order to work on his models or draw because that was when the house was quiet and he had some space and time for himself. Miguel would often meet me at the door bleary-eyed and explain that he had stayed up late working on a model, tying flies, or drawing. He was particularly skilled at working intensively for short bursts of time and being able to put the work aside for sometimes a week or two. This way of being within his practice was particularly important because of his life circumstances. Miguel spent most of his energy and time taking care of his family and working to make money. Also, because of the fear he felt of getting arrested again, he was not able to practice his graffiti as freely as Gil and Ian could engage in their practices. This feeling of being restricted regarding his creative practices prompted Miguel to adapt his work and engage in multiple projects at the same time.

The e-mail in the beginning of this book that I quoted from Ian regarding putting his zine together is indicative of the ways in which many youth work: at all hours, on multiple tasks simultaneously, and idiosyncratically. Ian pieced his zines together on the floor of his bedroom while running back and forth to his computer to print things out or communicate with friends. In addition the youth determined what they were going to do in and through their work. In other words, through reflection they realized what sources they needed in and through the work in which they were engaged. Ian would initiate IM conversations while he worked on his zines as a way of reflecting on and discussing what he was trying to accomplish in the zine.

Another important characteristic of the work that Ian, Gil, and Miguel did was that when they came up against an insurmountable obstacle or were not satisfied with what they had done, they moved on. They may have put the work away and come back to it at another time or not. This meant that their work involved ongoing evaluation, experimentation, and partially completed projects. They had the freedom to determine when a project did not merit completion. For example, Miguel had several manila folders and sketchbooks filled with partially drawn pictures and quick sketches of ideas he had for graffiti pieces or tattoos. Ian's class notes for English were literally interrupted by a few lines of a poem that popped into his head, a sentence or two for a story he was creating, or a paragraph for a political rant he was constructing. Gil had a notebook in which he scribbled ideas for turntable pieces as well as records he wanted to obtain and names and contact information of people associated with turntablism. He also gave me several audiotapes of partially completed pieces.

These starts and stops on their own may not seem to amount to much, but when put together they actually enabled the youth to bring other projects within their practices to completion. These scraps of ideas, or moments of experimentation, were also evaluated by the youth with a set of unconscious or conscious criteria. This particular aspect of how youth work on their own terms can have direct implications for the way we teach because it turns upside down the idea that the goal in learning is the product as opposed to the process. Miguel, Ian, and Gil show that the accumulation of attempts that lead up to an eventual piece of graffiti, a collage, or a turntable composition are where we should focus our pedagogical attention if we want youth to produce powerful and meaningful work.

Instead of making everyone follow the same steps for a research paper, for example, teachers need to recognize everyone's personal way of exploring something by establishing a set of criteria that enables students to construct their own way of finding what it is they want to explore and how they want to explore it. One way of honoring this diversity is through providing multiple strategies for engaging in an activity. Instead of teaching one strategy for beginning a research paper, teachers can discuss six or seven different ways to begin. These strategies should come from an understanding of how historians go about finding what it is that they want to write about. Teachers should offer alternatives to the reified way of researching commonly promulgated in schools. A plethora of strategies communicates to students that the "school" way is not "the way," and that often one's way to research runs counter to what school has authorized.

While this example targets research, one could easily manipulate it and put it to use in any discipline. It is possible to alter it for science or math, for example, because the discussion speaks to *practice,* and these practices are shared across disciplines or fields of study. They are shared by professionals engaged in constructing knowledge in these fields. Specifically, providing multiple strategies encourages students to experiment, to reflect, to organize what they have already written and look for patterns, and to look back over what they have already written and see how they can build on it.

This kind of work discussion would not have the same kind of resonance unless the class was also engaged in ongoing conversations where teachers and students articulate to each other and themselves how they work. Like the craft conversations that Gil had with Sam and Rudolpho, Miguel had with Carlos, and Ian had with MarxNSparx, teachers and students need to build a database or repertoire of authentic tactics and strategies for doing the work of the class that comes from the ways in which youth work in the world and from the ways in which established historians, scientists, mathematicians, and writers engage in their respective crafts. This form of dialogue draws crucial parallels between the ways youth make meaning in their worlds and the way professionals engage in their crafts, helping youth see how they are budding young mathematicians, historians, scientists, and writers.

Working Alongside Our Students

Gil, Ian, and Miguel surrounded themselves with others who were engaged in the same or a similar practice. Certainly there were times when these three worked on their craft by themselves, but a lot of their time was spent with others either in the act of doing the creative practice or talking about it. This meant that when they got together, they were speaking from a collective work/learning experience. Miguel worked with his brother on tattoos. Ian assembled groups of friends in order to publish his zines. Gil played with and watched Del and others work on the turntables. These communities of practice introduced new skills to be developed, books to read, movies to see, words to learn, places to go, and concepts to understand.

Too often in classrooms, teachers *present* work and the last thing that the teacher would ever consider is doing that work *along* with her students. In this case, the teacher positions herself as an interpreter of the work or as a "specialist," to use Said's term. This approach to learning contradicts the way youth, and I would argue professionals, do real work. Part of what makes Gil, Miguel, and Ian productive in their practices is the fact that their friends are actively engaged in the work as well. This egalitarian approach to the work provides a shared language in which the youth can communicate as well as a set of rituals and behaviors that are commonly understood. It also generates an atmosphere of productivity that can be infectious.

Certainly, Dewey advocates for this kind of engaged pedagogy when he writes that "the very nature of the work done [is] a social enterprise in which all individuals have an opportunity to contribute and to which all feel a responsibility" (1997, p. 56). This way of working resonates with people like Kirby, Kirby, and Liner, who suggest that writing teachers are readers and writers "modeling the life of a literate person" (Kirby, Kirby, & Liner, 2003, p. 10). Foxfire's core practices include "[t]he work teachers and learners do together is infused from the beginning with learner choice, design, and revision....The role of the teacher is that of facilitator and collaborator" (Hatton, 2004, p. 140). Lave and Wenger argue that learners develop enduring understandings through "participat[ing] in communities of practitioners and that the mastery of knowledge and skill require newcomers to move toward full participation in the sociocultural practices of a community" (1991, p. 29). According to Lave and Wenger, if we as teachers want our students to master certain knowledge and skills, a culture of work must be constructed where the teacher is involved in the work—"sociocultural practices"—of the class as opposed to being an outside observer of those practices.

We have somehow lost this idea in middle and secondary schools for the most part. It is a rare classroom space where the teacher collaborates with the students. What I commonly see in classrooms are math teachers presenting predetermined math problems or hands-on activities and having students figure them out; history teachers lecturing on specific times or historical figures; science teachers either lecturing on a specific scientific concept, showing a predetermined experiment, or monitoring students engaged in a predetermined science experiment; or English teachers monitoring their students as they write or interpret literature. All of these examples illustrate how the teacher is in the role of overseer instead of collaborator, an interpreter instead of appropriator.

As a seventh- and eighth-grade teacher, I would sometimes be invited to area universities to talk with teacher certification students about the work that I did with my students. I would make it a point to bring along several of my students, believing that they could talk more powerfully and convincingly about our work than I ever could. One time stands out for me. At one point in the discussion, a certification student asked my students, "What do you think you will remember about Mr. G's class?" One of my students leaned forward in his chair and said that he would remember how I always did the work with them. He went on to say that he had never had a teacher that did that before, and for him, that changed everything in the class. It made him work harder. Another student added that because I did the work with them, it made the work seem more important, more real.

These responses to the question surprised me. I fully expected them to talk about a particular story they had written or when we watched *Romeo and Juliet* or a particular field trip we went on. It also surprised me because I did not do the work with them thinking it would be some kind of pedagogical strategy for getting them to do the work. I had done the work with them because I was interested in it myself. I wanted to write with them. I wanted to act with them. I wanted to get their feedback on my work. It wasn't until that presentation that I realized that simply doing the work with my students was an incredibly powerful teaching tool.

We need to write with our students, do scientific experiments with our students, and research alongside our students. This way of being a teacher goes beyond modeling how we would like students to work and learn. Often modeling in classrooms is used simply to show students what to do or how to do something. It does not stem from real work that the teacher is engaged in. The modeling does not come from an intrinsic way of being a mathematician, historian, scientist, or writer in front of our students. Instead, we need to be personally interested in the work. The modeling, then, is done not just to show students what to do but also to actually help us continue the work. We need to *learn* within our classrooms. With that, we need to engage in conversations with our students around what it means to work and how we do it. This discourse is a fundamental part of how youth work in the everyday.

I am reminded of the conversation Miguel and his brother had as he got his tattoo. While on the surface this vignette may be read as a painful experience, underneath we can see the sophisticated conversation that they construct around books they read, films they watch, the meaning of family, and the technical skill of creating a tattoo in this way. Miguel participated in this sociocultural practice with his brother. He was an apprentice of sorts, watching his brother work in front of him and learning the craft alongside him.

The classroom should be a space of mutual work. Instead of the traditional "detached spectatorship" where the teacher observes, interprets, and evaluates the learning of students, we need to shift to a classroom space of actors—with both students and teachers engaged in the challenges, frustrations, and benefits of real work. This shift requires us to understand ourselves as historians, scientists, mathematicians, and writers in our everyday lives. It necessitates having passions that we want to pursue and share with our students. By shifting into an embodied practice of teaching, our classrooms become spaces where learning happens for real and present reasons for both the teacher and the students.

BUILDING A CLASSROOM INFRASTRUCTURE THROUGH QUESTIONS

Thus far, I discussed how teachers can position themselves as ethnographers and amateurs in order to develop understandings of how their students work on their own terms. I then made connections between developing an ethnographic understanding and designing learning environments, focusing specifically on building into a classroom infrastructure multiple forms of performance and experimentation, idiosyncratic work processes, and working alongside students. In order to make that connection, I recalled how Gil, Miguel, and Ian worked in their daily lives in turntablism, graffiti, tattooing, and zine writing. I also posited several scenarios illustrating what a classroom would look, sound, and feel like if it were influenced by youth ways of working. Now I would like to place these rituals and routines in a larger curriculum design that would encourage and support these youth ways of working.

I and others call this design a "curriculum infrastructure" (see Appelbaum, in press; Gustavson & Appelbaum, 2005). The idea of a "curriculum infrastructure" is informed by inquiry-based learning (IBL). Therefore, to begin this conversation, I will briefly describe IBL and then outline how to build an infrastructure that supports IBL and echoes the habits of mind and body that enable youth to do work on their own terms in classroom spaces. Throughout I draw from the ways Gil, Ian, and Miguel work—as illustrated in the preceding chapters—to show the congruity between youth learning on their own terms and IBL.

Inquiry-Based Learning

There is an abundance of resources and research on IBL and teaching: what it is (Barell, 1998), the theory behind it (Dewey, 1966; Wiggins, 1991), the history behind it (Kleibard, 1986), and how to do it (Daniels & Bizar, 1998; Polamn, 2000; Starnes & Paris, 2000; Wolf, 1987). Books, journals, Web sites, and yearly conferences are dedicated to discussing and exploring this way of learning (see http://ilf.crlt.indiana.edu/). Every major professional teaching organization (NCTE, NCTM, NCST, NCSST, NSTA) advocates IBL. District curricular mandates also suggest that students should learn through inquiry. However, amid this overwhelming support for inquiry as a "method" for learning, seeming to come from all ends of the educational spectrum, in my experience as a teacher and teacher educator fewer and fewer teachers see IBL as a way to design rigorous and personally meaningful work and learning in their classrooms. More specifically, teachers have a difficult time merging IBL with scripted curricula.

With the pre-service and in-service teachers with whom I work, inquiry is often a new idea. They never experienced it before—not as an elementary, middle, or secondary student—and certainly not in their other education classes or professional development workshops.

Because of this inability to draw from their personal experience with inquiry, students and teachers with whom I work treat inquiry as a radical and new concept. Many express excitement about the possibility of teaching through inquiry but at the same time do not see how they could possibly do "this kind of thing" in their own classrooms because of standardized curricula and testing. They also do not make the immediate link between IBL and the ways in which youth specifically, and all people more generally, learn on their own terms. In other words, they do not see how IBL as a mode of learning *is* the way we learn in our everyday lives, namely through large and small questions that we ask and then pursue in a multitude of ways.

Inquiry-based learning is a complex opportunity for exploration and authentic problem solving that evolves from a theme or issue. It begins with identifying essential questions around broad intellectual topics that are either asked by teachers or by students. These questions do not have definitive answers and cannot be answered with "yes" or "no." Instead, students and teachers *explore* the questions through varied and rigorous means, discover other questions along the way, and ultimately come to an educated perspective on the original question. E. W. Eisner describes this process of learning as "expressive objectives." "It identifies a situation in which youth are to work, a problem with which they are to cope, a task in which they are to engage; but it does not specify what from that encounter, situation, problem, or task they are to learn" (Goodson, 1998, p. 34). Through this process, students and teachers develop particular skills and conceptual knowledge that enable them to explore their questions. Inquiry is often depicted as a circular process where one asks a series of embedded questions, investigates those questions, constructs an answer to those questions, discusses the findings, and reflects on the work. The student then asks the next question—often spurred by the previous inquiry—and starts the process again.

In a class designed around the rituals, routines, and practices of inquiry, teachers and students use time to explore their own questions around broad intellectual topics. Goodson writes, "The teacher helps the child isolate a problem that is puzzling him...together they devise a plan for investigating the problems, the investigation promotes a number of hypotheses, these are worked through and reformulated, and together the teacher and child discuss and define a mutually acceptable solution" (1998, p. 37). Most often these kinds of questions are explored through interviewing, text-based research, experiments for hard science questions and math-related projects, reflective writing, observations, and trial and error.

There comes a time in this process when the students and the teachers learn enough to be able to make something out of the knowledge. For example, students may take the knowledge that they have constructed around strip mining and its environmental impact to the state legislature to encourage legislators to pass a law regulating the practice. A student pursuing questions about atonal musical compositions may create his own composition. A student's more complex understanding of the genocide in Darfur may lead her to establish a student group whose focus is raising awareness of the humanitarian crisis. The general idea is that the knowledge that one constructs through this process is not only for the purpose of the classroom, the teacher, or even the student herself. The knowledge that one constructs needs to be put back out into the world where others can benefit from it. There are real-world implications for the work that students are doing within IBL.

The process of inquiry does not stop there, however. After students and teachers have created something out of their work and have taken action on that work in the world, students and teachers then discuss the knowledge they have constructed. They evaluate what they have learned and what it means for them. They discuss what happened when they put what they learned back out into the world. What surprised them? What did they learn through taking action on their inquiry? What would they do differently the next time? What questions did it raise?

The final phase of the inquiry process is reflecting on the experience as a whole, making explicit the skills and conceptual knowledge that teachers and students developed through the inquiry. In this phase, teachers often bring out the performance objectives outlined by their districts and design activities and workshops where groups of students connect the work and learning that they did within their inquiries to the skill and concept goals of the district-mandated curriculum (see Starnes & Paris, 2000). Teachers will literally take out their performance objectives, as outlined in their core curriculum, and ask the students, "What standards did you meet through your inquiry, and how did you meet them?" Standards that are seemingly not met are discussed and addressed. In this phase, teachers will also design challenges where students must take the knowledge that they have constructed through their inquiries and apply it to new or seemingly unrelated problems. This phase ends with students and teachers identifying the next question they want to pursue, the next project they want to get involved in, or the next problem that they want to explore. This step in the final phase is guided by the expectations of the curriculum.

IBL is not a singular method for teaching. Perhaps the most familiar mode of inquiry in classrooms is the Socratic method. The Socratic method is a teaching strategy whereby the teacher *leads* the student to an understanding or conclusion through a series of often predetermined questions known by the teacher. When done well, the teacher does not offer any answers. Instead, each question is answered with another question. However, these questions are limited in their scope because of the predetermined answer that the teacher is leading the student to. Discovery or understanding in this case is completely controlled by the teacher. As we have seen through the work of Miguel, Ian, and Gil, the Socratic method is not generally part of the ways in which youth work on their own terms. It is rare that youth rely on an authority figure to be the source or way to knowledge. Instead, youth like Miguel, Gil, and Ian have a more diverse strategy for constructing knowledge about their craft. They look to adults or to peers who are in the practice; they hang out in spaces where their creative practice is being performed; they read. Through this multiplicity of sources, youth ask their own questions and come to know their craft.

Two other common ways of structuring IBL is through a problem-based approach or a project-based approach. With problem-based learning, the impetus for exploration comes from a problem that has been identified, which, through exploring it, would enable students to develop specific skills and conceptual knowledge relevant to the discipline. These problems are "ill-structured," meaning that the answers to them are not readily apparent and that the work involved to "answer" them is "open-ended and complex enough to require collaboration and thinking beyond recall" (see http://ctl.stanford.edu/Newsletter/problem_based_learning.pdf). With project-based learning, an idea for a project—something that needs to be built, drawn, designed, implemented—is the goal of the unit. What connects these different ways of doing IBL are the questions that need to be asked to either explore the problem or do the project as well as their focus on designing learning experiences that build on students' interests, that connect to the "real world," and that provide opportunities to develop essential disciplinary skills and conceptual knowledge.

IBL shifts the set of responsibilities for students and teachers within the classroom. The focus is taken away from the teacher being the interpreter of knowledge. Instead, the teachers' primary role is to design class time to appropriate habits of mind and body that enable students to explore these essential questions that they have identified. Instead of preparing a set of lectures before the class starts, teachers who design IBL experiences think more about the kind of work that students are going to do both in and out of their classrooms in order to pursue the problems and projects—and questions within both—that interest the students. Teachers should have a deep sense of the practice behind being a mathematician, scientist, historian, or writer and understand that the work of the class should encourage their students to *be* these kinds of people.

Teachers work to design specific criteria for the work that communicates to the students what is valued within the class and provides an infrastructure for doing meaningful work. Within IBL, teachers often describe themselves as facilitators, coaches, or collaborators in the learning experience. The teacher is a resource for the students, never withholding the knowledge that she has regarding the topic being explored, but having faith in the capacities of her students to explore the questions. IBL teachers tune in to the appropriate times for providing information or insight that will deepen learning. They provide specific, disciplinary language to the processes and concepts that students develop. They help to make explicit the connection between the work of the class and curricular expectations. In Wiggins's (1989) words, a teacher "enables students, at any level, to see how knowledge grows out of, resolves, and produces questions" (p. 45).

Through setting up an infrastructure that enables students to work on their own terms within the classroom, teachers can spend their time in more meaningful ways: pursuing their own inquiries, identifying appropriate times when direct instruction is needed, finding patterns between different questions, setting up individual or small group conferences with students, modeling work, etc. In essence, teachers who design inquiry-based classrooms embody what it means to *be* a mathematician, scientist, historian, or writer for and with their students.

Curriculum as Infrastructure

This kind of pedagogical work can only happen when teachers design their courses as *infrastructures* for work and learning as opposed to *structures*. By curriculum infrastructure, I mean the rituals, routines, activities, forms of evaluation and assessment, and criteria that make it possible for specific kinds of work and learning to happen. An infrastructure shows students what they have the freedom to do within an identified intellectual boundary often taking the form of a discipline like American literature, biology, ancient history, or algebra, for example.

This pedagogical stance of thinking of the inner workings of one's course as an *infrastructure* contrasts with what I would argue is the more common design choice of creating structures for work. Curriculum as structure, in Dewey's (1966) words, "demands an internal consistency of parts in connection with one another." He continues to say that structures make possible *only* what already exists. In other words, when we design learning environments as structures, the potential for learning only exists in what is delivered by the teacher. The Socratic method is a structural form for inquiry. There is an imposed path that the student is to take in order to come to expected conclusions. Lectures are often designed as structures. The teacher speaks to one way of understanding the Cuban Missile Crisis, thus implying that our understanding of this complicated event in history already exists, positioning students as spectators of history as opposed to actors engaged in constructing new understandings of past events. Tests and quizzes are examples of curricular structures as well. Their form—a series of questions to be answered about a particular topic—implies that there is a predetermined set of facts that define a piece of literature, scientific concept, or historical event.

I am not suggesting that lectures, tests, and quizzes are ipso facto *structural*. Like any method of teaching, they are a function of design. One could just as easily draft a lecture or test that supported students asking questions and developing their own ideas and conclusions. Dewey (1960) warns that a structural orientation to work and learning separates "intellect from action…knowing over doing and making." Curriculum as structure positions students as *students* of math, science, history, or English. This view of the learner limits the role of the student to someone who consumes information and regurgitates it for the teacher. He or she is a spectator in the learning process. Other seemingly more important people have done the work of exploring the idea, identifying the problem, or understanding the issue. Finally, like Said's argument for the amateur over the specialist, Dewey suggests that curriculum as structure makes it difficult to see what could be known outside of the parameters of the structure. He uses the analogy of the human eye: Because it is what we see through, it is impossible to imagine what perfect sight could *look* like.

Conversely, curriculum as infrastructure positions students *as* mathematicians, scientists, historians, and writers. They create mathematical languages to describe their findings. They design and perform their own experiments to test a hypothesis. They conduct interviews, interpret primary documents, and develop their own theories. They write their own poems, short stories, and novels. They work in classrooms the way most of them work on their own terms in their daily lives.

Gil, Miguel, and Ian pursue their own ideas and questions within their creative practices. They are constantly in the act of devising new problem-solving strategies to overcome particular challenges. Miguel, Ian, and Gil collaborate on a regular basis with their communities of practice. They reflect on their work. They represent their art forms in diverse ways. Finally, they construct authentic and ongoing forms of evaluation and assessment to determine the efficacy of their work. I have inferred throughout this discussion of IBL and curriculum as infrastructure that the ways in which the youth within this book work and learn on their own terms closely resembles the ways students are encouraged to work and learn through IBL. This isn't surprising because IBL as pedagogy takes its cue from how children and youth learn in the everyday. Dewey emphatically states that when it comes to how we should be thinking about designing learning environments, "The case is of the Child. It is his present powers which are to assert themselves; his present capacities which are to be exercised; his present attitudes which are to be realized" (1966, p. 31). William Reinsmith adds:

> Students will learn only what they have some proclivity for or interest in. Find out what a person likes, then help him build around it. Once interest exists learning is possible, and teaching kicks in. We waste enormous quantities of time (and money) giving students learning tasks for which they have no interest or readiness, boring them and frustrating ourselves in the process. This is one of the tragic defects of mass education. (1997, p. 7)

Lemke suggests:

> We learn in activities, but more fully in networks of activities that are interdependent of one another, that facilitate and enable one another, that are marked out as being relevant to understanding each other's meanings. These networks are constructed differently by different groups, and to some extent also by different individuals, not only in what we say are relevant connections, but in what we make to be relevant connections by how we act and what we do, and sometimes by the very fact of our lives bridging these networks together. (1997, p. 52)

According to Lemke, youth specifically, and people more broadly, learn through combinations of activities and groups of people. These networks create connections of meaning that make it possible for meaningful work to get accomplished. These connections do not just happen. Lemke suggests that people work to make these connections and act in certain ways within these networks in order for them to be relevant and useful. These networks are interdependent of one another. It is the connections between activities that enrich the learning within the individual activities. I see IBL as a process for finding out what our students are interested in and building learning experiences around their present powers and capacities.

CONCLUSION: MAKING OUR CLASSROOMS YOUTHSPACES

Dewey articulates the challenge of redesigning our classrooms to implicitly and explicitly honor youth work in this way:

> Abandon the notion of subject-matter as something fixed and ready-made in itself, outside the child's experience; cease thinking of the child's experience as also something hard and fast; see it as something fluent, embryonic, vital; and we realize that the child and the curriculum are simply two limits which define a single process. (1966, p. 11)

In this quote, Dewey pushes us to challenge the prevailing feeling that our disciplines are predetermined by mandated curricula and divorced from the *lives* of youth; to find the links between curricula and the way children learn in their everyday lives; to look at both curricula and children's lives as flexible and malleable. When we do this, Dewey argues, a child's experience and the curriculum are complementary. Throughout this book, I have argued that when educators investigate and acknowledge the creative practices of youth within their pedagogy, opportunities for authentic learning emerge: teachers tune their teaching practices more closely to the ways in which youth learn and make meaning in their everyday lives; they heed the call of writers-educators like Maxine Greene who encourage us to make the ways in which students work and learn in their everyday lives explicit in their teaching. She writes:

> To engage with our students as persons is to affirm our own incompleteness, our consciousness of spaces still to be explored, desires still to be tapped, possibilities still to be opened and pursued....We have to find out how to open such spheres, such spaces, where a better state of things can be imagined....I would like to think that this can happen in classrooms, in corridors, in schoolyards, in the streets. (1986, p. 29)

An ethnographic understanding of the ways in which youth perform, experiment, reflect, form communities of practice, evaluate, and interpret within their daily lives allows us to treat students as people with "desires still to be tapped, possibilities still to be opened and pursued." In classroom environments driven by prepackaged curricula or standardized testing, students are figured as finite and closed systems, lacking essential skills and knowledge. These classrooms lack the open-ended fluidity of authentic, meaningful learning and fail to acknowledge the disciplinary strengths that youth bring with them, regardless of background. They make it difficult for students and teachers to develop a shared sense of *how they can learn together*. One way of weaving into the fabric of the class habits of mind and body that are at the heart of the work that Gil, Miguel, Ian, and so many youth choose to do is through developing classroom infrastructures informed by inquiry-based learning. Indeed, IBL honors the *personhood* of each of our students and provides an opportunity to reframe traditional questions like "How can I [teacher] teach them [students] these skill and concept objectives?" to "How can we as a community of practice develop these skills and concepts, utilizing my [teacher] understanding of the creative intelligence at work in my students' daily lives?"

While this reframing may seem insignificant, in fact, it opens up the possibility of adopting curricular standards as a guide rather than as a set of constraints to be slavishly followed. In this light, curricular standards are not the source of the problem as many teachers feel. Rather, they become useful tools for learning. We can then work with our students to meet the current high-stakes testing curriculum in the same ways these students meet challenges in the work of their daily lives—by implementing what I have discussed above as authentic forms of performance, experimentation, reflection, interpretation, and evaluation. Through this recasting of teacher and student roles as well as how learning looks, sounds, and feels, we transform the classroom into a *youthspace* where youth ways of knowing are embraced and put to work.

I wrote this book in part to honor the myriad ways youth create meaning in and through creative practices. I argue for a close and rigorous examination of the different aspects of youth creative practices, to deepen the understanding of the crucial roles these practices play in the larger context of learning. I also wrote this book with the belief that youth can and should play a significant role in educating us as teachers. The way Miguel, Ian, and Gil form communities of practice, perform, experiment, reflect, evaluate, and interpret in and through their practices complicates what is often considered legitimate forms of work and learning in classrooms. Sometimes youth, like Ian, when faced with this contrast, find ways to sneak their practices into school, flying under the curricular radar, so to speak. Or, like Gil, they will be lucky enough to find spaces outside of academic classes to engage in their practices. At other times, youth will opt out, making the choice to continue their practices outside of school. In the case of Miguel, he dropped out of school. This decision was not solely based on the incongruity between his creative practice and the school's way of practicing learning. However, it played a role.

The stories of Miguel, Ian, and Gil represent what most youth desire: control over their own learning trajectories. They want and need to work and learn on their own terms. Some youth do this through a refusal to attend school altogether; others make school a part of their wider learning worlds. They recognize the interdependence of the role school plays with other learning spaces. School does not occupy a monolithic position, separate from the rest of their lives. The creative practices of Gil, Miguel, and Ian show how the dominant representation of school as the center of a youth's learning world, in the mass media and educational policy, is too reductive and static.

Perhaps going to school would not be such an alienating endeavor to many youth if adults in positions of power recognized and valued the many ways youth learn on their own terms. Perhaps by recognizing the role creative practices play in how youth learn, administrators, teachers, parents, and students can find ways to weave the sophisticated work processes of youth with the learning objectives of school. Then school can be a viable and essential space through which youth and adults can learn together.

APPENDIX: RESEARCHING WITH
MIGUEL, GIL, AND IAN

Conducting ethnographic research involves issues of relationship building. Put simply, the data come from spending prolonged amounts of time with participants in particular contexts. It is in and through the relationships that a researcher has with participants that the researcher develops an understanding of a phenomenon. However, as Marcus (1998) reminds us, field relations are slippery and at best tenuous. In other words, "good" relationships do not simply equal "meaningful" data or research. Furthermore, ethnographic research does not identify a truth regarding a phenomenon. Rather, through the act of research, participants and researcher construct a new culture in and through which phenomena are partially understood (Clifford & Marcus, 1986; Marcus, 1998). Schultz (1999) suggests that conducting research with youth is particularly challenging with respect to the issue of building relationships. Often researcher and participants are at cross-purposes with respect to the research. In addition, the disparity in age between the researcher and participants can make this kind of work difficult. An adult researcher can be a "double outsider" in terms of age and lack of understanding of particular ways of being as a youth.

The challenges inherent in relationship building in ethnographic research were particularly salient for my research. Issues of race and class permeated the relationships I had with Miguel, Ian, and Gil. These relationships were incredibly complicated. I was cognizant, for example, of the way in which Miguel managed or controlled a particular kind of research space. I remember a particular time when he and I had planned to meet. I arrived at his house to find Miguel asleep on the mattress on the living room floor. His cousin answered the door when I knocked, opening the door a crack. Peering around Miguel's cousin, I could see Miguel sleeping on the air mattress behind her. I told his cousin that I was there to see Miguel. When she went to tell Miguel that I was there, he told her that he was sleeping and did not want to get up. She came back to the door and relayed the information that I had heard and then closed the door. I stood there for a minute, looking at Miguel's motionless body on the mattress through the window in the door. I then called through the door, "Come on, Miguel." He remained still. I could only imagine how foolish I must have looked. After a few seconds, I turned and made my way back to the car. I remember driving back home frustrated and hurt because it had taken me over an hour to get to his house, and we had planned to spend the entire day together; hurt because I could not help feeling that this in some way was an indication of how important our relationship was to him.

Later, I realized that this situation illustrated the complications of doing research. On the one hand, I understood Miguel's refusal to get up as an indication that he was tired from waking up early and working until late at night the day before. On the other hand, I think it was also a direct way of reminding me that research is a process of negotiation. In a sense, we would not work unless Miguel wanted us to work. On yet another level, this scene reminded me of the relative importance of the research in relation to his work and struggles as someone living and working in poverty.

Gil and I negotiated the research as well. One time I called Gil to ask him if I could go to church with him. Gil said he was not sure. He said, "You know that the church is mostly black, right?" I remember sitting on the phone in our kitchen and wondering where Gil was coming from with that statement. His reasons for me not coming along sounded cobbled together, spontaneous. I responded rather feebly, "I've been to black churches before." Surely he knew me well enough to know that the ethnic makeup of the church did not concern me. Off balance, I caught myself thinking, "Is he implying I'm racist?" Not sure what to do with that thought, I pushed it aside and trudged onward: "Are you sure I can't go?" Gil said, "Yeah, but it's a bit awkward." I asked him why and he said rather abruptly, "You're not a Christian and you don't believe what I believe." After a long pause, the only response I could muster was, "What do you mean?"

Gil talked about how it was awkward for me to go to church with him when I did not believe in it. I tried to explain that I am a spiritual person and that I did not judge him because of his religious beliefs. Gil challenged my statement by referring to a time when I apparently made a joke about Jesus Christ. I told him that I could not remember the joke, but that I was sorry for telling it. He understood that I apologized but he said, "It's harder to forget." He said that it goes beyond the joke I made.

"Leif," Gil said, "we're coming from two completely different places." He added that he felt at times that I did not agree with the decisions that he makes. "Like where I go on the weekends, or what kind of music I listen to," he said. Where did this come from? I felt as if I tried very hard to not be judgmental. Gil and I had a four-year history with one another. I taught him in seventh grade, and we kept in touch after I left the school to go back and get my degree. I was not just a researcher and an adult, I was also a teacher to Gil. I was coming to realize that this history was a lot of baggage to carry around. The research that Gil and I were doing was not simply built on the flimsy infrastructure of that relationship. It started with a questionable and complicated foundation of previous experiences we had shared and of larger societal constructs that permeate personal relationships.

All these factors contributed to Gil's unease that evening on the phone. He felt like he had little control over the research and because of that he was afraid that he was either going to be the "ass of a joke," as he liked to put it, or misrepresented. He expressed concern that he did not have control over what I saw as a "researcher"; that by telling the truth, he may incriminate himself. Gil also admitted to the fact that he did not always want to tell the truth.

He went back into our personal history and brought up the example of me misstating where he came from as well as his family's economic status in a paper he and I worked on a few years before. He took great pains to explain to me that I had built a text about him entirely on assumptions. "How do I know that you aren't going to do that again?" Gil asked.

The list of mistakes became a litany. I was riding a wave of errors. These waves did not come uniformly. Instead, they crashed into each other unpredictably. At one point in the conversation, he said that he thought I was on the ball but that I made a lot of mistakes just like everyone else does. "Society makes it difficult for us to bring up stuff like relationships, feelings, and issues of power," Gil said. Gil continued to bring up examples, qualifying at the end, "I don't hold this stuff against you, but these things offend me."

What made this conversation even more difficult for me was Gil's understanding tone. It would have been much easier to deal with his criticism had he simply berated me or blown the research into thin air, but he tempered his well-grounded concerns with a genuine care for the relationship.

As the conversation wound down, I said, "I'm really sorry," and thanked Gil for the talk. I admitted that it was a serious blow to my self-confidence, but I thought it was important. Gil said, "You don't need to apologize, man. Self-confidence is based on stuff you are supposed to know, Leif."

Even Ian, with whom I thought I had a close relationship, marked the relational space between us by mentioning every so often how difficult it was not to think of me as his teacher—a wrinkle in the research that proved quite fruitful for exploring what meaningful teacher-student work relationships could be.

I do not want to give the impression that the youth and I were at odds throughout the research. On the contrary, Miguel, Gil, Ian, and I worked together to find personal and communal reasons for doing the research. I offer these glimpses into the backstage dealings of the field-work as a way to express my understanding of the youth's lives broadly and their creative practices specifically as partial. Through a process of negotiation, the youth and I constructed one way of making meaning. Without a doubt, there are many other ways as well.

With these research relationships being so complicated, I have wondered about how to represent my findings. How can I acknowledge the complexity of the ways in which we constructed the research? The most appropriate way to acknowledge the complexity and change inherent in this research is to make tentative assertions about my findings. This process of meaning making draws from Cintron's (1997) notion of the blending of ethos—one's "moral character or disposition"—with logos—a "rational argument." He writes:

> Indeed, rationality, the pure kind, does not exist outside the soup of human affairs. In matters of persuasion, then, character plays an important role. In some cases, one might even say that the carefully deliberated argument is itself a sign of character. However configured, the central point is that ethos and logos—or character and a rational knowledge claim—are linked so that knowing something of a person's character helps us to judge that person's knowledge claims. We can say this more enigmatically: logos is layered with ethos and ethos is layered with logos. (p. 3)

I find Cintron's point to be particularly relevant when one researches the everyday creative practices of youth. Often, representations of youth in academic research, the mass media, and even teachers' lounges have been everything but hopeful and positive. Giroux (1996) writes, "Youth cultures are often viewed in the popular press as aberrant, unpredictable, and dangerous in terms of the investments they produce, social relations they affirm, and the anti-politics they sometimes legitimate" (p. 11). Mike Males's (1999) powerful deconstruction of the media's misrepresentation of youth culture clearly shows that often the media frames youth as the source for much of what is wrong with society today. Perhaps Heath (1999) speaks most clearly of this kind of (mis)representation in academic research particularly when it comes to writing about urban youth living in poverty:

> No group under the scrutiny of social scientists has been more heavily over-generalized than urban teens who live in impoverished neighborhoods. From developmentalists to clinicians to educators, justice officials, and the popular media, adults have made universal and predominantly negative claims about the behaviors and attitudes of those in the second decade of their lives who live in these communities. Much of this research forms the basis of remediation or intervention programs designed to correct or improve teens who live in underserved neighborhoods with substantial crime rates, few opportunities for employment, and underfunded schools. This is not to say that there have not been books that both document and celebrate the lives of individual teens from troubled neighborhoods....But these stories invariably suggest that only by managing to separate themselves from their own communities can individual teens succeed. (p. 1)

I do not want to contribute to this form of oppression through the way in which I entextualize Miguel, Ian, and Gil. Instead, I seek to represent the "soup of human affairs" that defines this research and is a part of the lives of the youth in this study. I do this not as a prescription but as a way to value who the youth are and the work that they do.

Concern over the issue of representation in ethnographic research is not new (Anzaldua, 1987; Behar, 1996; Clifford & Marcus, 1986; hooks, 1994; Lather & Smithies, 1997; Marcus, 1998). Marcus (1998) stresses that a researcher's findings are in fact a construction of the thoughts and feelings of many and should be represented as such. Behar (1996) is concerned with what she calls the "oxymoron" of participant observation:

> [A]ct as a participant, but don't forget to keep your eyes open... when the grant money runs out, or the summer vacation is over, please stand up, dust yourself off, go to your desk, and write down what you saw and heard. Relate it to something you've read by Marx, Weber, Gramsci, or Geertz and you're on your way to doing anthropology. (p. 5)

Recognizing the inherent ironies in speaking for the many through one voice and becoming involved in the lives of others only to later step away and write about them, I want to invoke Marcus's (1998) "messy text" as a way of facing these ironies. His notion of the "messy text" speaks to my hesitancy to pass judgment on the youth as well as my desire to include the "mundanity" of their everyday lives as crucial information for teachers. Marcus lays out several reasons for making texts "messy" in ethnography. Two of them resonate particularly with my project and me. He writes:

> These texts wrestle with the loss of a credible holism, so important in previous ethnographic writing, especially functionalist accounts. In messy texts, there is a sense of a whole, without an evocation of totality, that emerges from the research process itself. The territory that defines the object of study is mapped by an ethnographer who is within its landscape, moving and acting within it rather than being drawn in from a transcendent, detached point.
>
> Messy texts are messy because they insist on their own open-endedness, incompleteness, and uncertainty about how to draw a text/analysis to a close. Such open-endedness often marks a concern with an ethics of dialogue and partial knowledge, a sense that work is incomplete without critical, and differently positioned, responses to it by its (ideally) varied readers. (pp. 188–189)

I see Marcus's call for the "messy text" not as a prescription for dealing with representing others. Instead, it is more of a metaphor that orients the reader and writer in terms of how the ethnographer is going to deal with the fact that one's findings are partial and incomplete. Certainly, my work is incomplete. While I have a relatively long history with Gil and Ian—I taught them and have maintained contact with them in varied forms for more than seven years now—the work that I did with them is still partial if only to say that I am not them and therefore it is impossible for me to speak to their creative practices from within them. While there are many ways in which I have strived to develop a deep and broad picture of the three youth's lives and work—by spending a prolonged amount of time with them in a variety of spaces and by involving them in the construction and representation of their creative practices and lives on paper—lives are complicated, perhaps too complicated to capture in a text.

In many ways, instead of the research providing answers to how youth learn and work on their own terms, it created more questions. It identified the multitude of spaces of which I know little or nothing about. Therefore, this text does not represent some form of concrete "reality." It is "the perception of reality" (Cintron, 1997, p. 5). It is my perception of reality filtered through my ethos. It is, as Lather and Smithies (1997) put it, "a threshold between what [I] know and what is beyond [my] knowing....[It is] about the limits of what can be said and known about the lives of others" (p. xiv).

The kind of ethnography I am trying to practice finds its strength in the texts I construct, texts that strive to move the reader through social criticism. Behar (1996) states, "When you write vulnerably, others respond vulnerably" (p.16). Denzin (1997) adds, "The ethnographer's tale is always allegorical—a symbolic tale that is not just a record of human experience for the reader. It is a vehicle for readers to discover moral truths about themselves. More deeply, the ethnographic tale... brings a moral compass back into the reader's (and the writer's) life" (pp. xiv–xv).

This ethnographic tale has certainly reoriented me in terms of my research with youth broadly and my teaching more specifically. I have come to understand Ian's, Miguel's, and Gil's ways of negotiating the research as a lesson in resisting the urge to nail down who they are and what they do. Ironically, this attention to flux and openness when working with youth creates avenues for understanding and social justice. I have come to see the process of negotiation in the research relationship as a way into the subtle nuances of their lives and work. I understand now that Ian, Miguel, and Gil see themselves as much more than a zine writer, turntablist, or graffiti writer. I am also aware now of the partial knowledge that the youth have about me—who I am, what I am interested in, and what I care about. Often, as a teacher, I find myself feeling like I need to know all. I feel the need to get rid of uncertainty and partial knowledge. I feel like my role is to know things in totality. My work with these three youth has taught me that real learning takes place when we explore the world of the unknown together. This mutual exploration creates partial understandings that honor the autonomy and agency that youth seek and deserve when it comes to forming work relationships with adults.

REFERENCES

Anderson, B. (1983). *Imagined communities: Reflections on the origin and spread of nationalism.* London: Verso.

Anzaldua, G. (1987). *Borderlands: La frontera.* San Francisco, CA: aunt lute books.

Appelbaum, P. (in press). *Embracing mathematics: On becoming a teacher and changing with mathematics.* Mahwah, NJ: Lawrence Erlbaum Associates.

Aronowitz, S., & Giroux, H.A. (1993). *Education still under siege* (2nd ed.). Westport, CT: Bergen & Garvey.

Ayers, W. (1998). Teaching as an ethical enterprise. *Educational Forum, 63*(1), 52–57.

Barell, J. (1998). *PBL: An inquiry approach.* Arlington Heights, IL: Skylight Training and Publishing.

Baron, J. (2000, June 10). Off the train, onto the block. *The New York Times,* pp. B1, B6.

Behar, R (1996). *The vulnerable observer: Anthropology that breaks your heart.* Boston, MA: Beacon Press.

Bridgeland, J.M., DiIulio, Jr., J.J., & Morison, K.B. (2006). The silent epidemic. Civic Enterprises in association with Peter D. Hart Research Associates for the Bill and Melinda Gates Foundation.

Callahan, R. (1962). *Education and the cult of efficiency.* Chicago: University of Chicago Press.

Camitta, M. (1993). Vernacular writing: Varieties of literacy among Philadelphia high school students. In B. Street (Ed.), *Cross-cultural approaches to literacy* (chap. 9). Cambridge, UK: Cambridge University Press.

Castleman, C. (1982). *Getting up: Subway graffiti in New York.* Cambridge, MA: MIT Press.

Chepesiuk, R. (1997). The zine scene: Libraries preserve the latest trend in publishing. *American Libraries, 28*(2), 68–70.

Chu, J. (1997). Navigating the media environment: How youth claim a place through zines. *Social Justice, 24*(3), 71–85.

Cintron, R. (1997). *Angels' town: Chero ways, gang life, and rhetorics of the everyday.* Boston, MA: Beacon Press.

Clifford, J., & Marcus, G.E. (Eds.). (1986). *Writing culture: The poetics and politics of ethnography.* Berkeley, CA: University of California Press.

Conquergood, D. (1997). Street literacy. In J. Flood, S. B. Heath, & D. Lapp (Eds.), *Handbook of research on teaching literacy through the communicative and visual arts* (pp. 354–375). New York: Macmillan Library.

Daniels, H., & Bizar, M. (1998). *Methods that matter: Six structures for best practice classrooms.* York, ME: Stenhouse Publishers.

De Certeau, M. (1984). *The practice of everyday life.* Berkeley: University of California Press.

Denzin, N. K. (1997). *Interpretive ethnography: Ethnographic practices for the 21st century.* Thousand Oaks, CA: Sage.

Dewey, J. (1960). *The quest for certainty.* New York: Capricorn Books.

Dewey, J. (1966). *The child and the curriculum and the school and society.* Chicago: University of Chicago Press.

Dewey, J. (1997). *Experience and education.* New York: Macmillan.

Dufrenne, M. (1973). *The phenomenology of aesthetic experience.* Evanston, IL: Northwestern University Press.

Essl, K. (2006). Improvisation on "improvisation." Retrieved July 2006 from http://www.essl.at/bibliogr/improvisation-e.html

Ferrell, J. (1995). Urban graffiti: Crime, control, and resistance. *Youth & Society, 27*(1), 73–92.

Foucault, M. (1995). *Discipline and punish: The birth of the prison* (2nd ed.). New York: Vintage.

Gallas, K. (1994). *The languages of learning: How children talk, write, dance, draw, and sing their understanding of the world.* New York: Teachers College Press.

Ganz, N., & McDonald, N. (2006). *Graffiti women: Street art from five continents.* New York: Harry N. Abrams.

George, N. (1998). *Hip hop America.* New York: Penguin.

Giroux, H.A. (1996). *Fugitive cultures: Race, violence, & youth.* New York: Routledge.

Goffman, E. (1990). *The presentation of self in everyday life.* New York: Anchor.

Goodson, I.F. (1998). Towards an alternative pedagogy. In J.L. Kincheloe & S.R. Steinberg (Eds.), *Unauthorized methods: Strategies for critical teaching* (chap. 2). New York: Routledge.

Goswami, D., & Stillman, P. (1987). *Reclaiming the classroom: Teacher research as an agency for change.* Upper Montclair, NJ: Boynton/Cook.

Greene, M. (1986). In search of a critical pedagogy. *Harvard Educational Review, 56*(4), 427–441.

Gross, D. M. (1994). Zine but not heard. *Time, 68*(2), 144.

Gunderloy, M., & Goldberg, C. (Eds.). (1990). *The world of zines: A guide to the independent magazine revolution.* New York: Penguin.

Gustavson, L., & Appelbaum, P. (2005). Youth cultural practices, popular culture, and classroom teaching. In J. Kincheloe (Ed.), *Classroom teaching: An introduction* (pp. 281–297). New York: Peter Lang.

Gustavson, L., & Cytrynbaum, J. (2003). Illuminating spaces: Relational spaces, complicity, and multisited ethnography. *Field Methods, 15,* 252–270.

Hager, S. (1984). *Hip hop: The illustrated history of break dancing, rap music, and graffiti.* New York: St. Martin's Press.

Hatton, S.D. (2004). *Teaching by heart: The Foxfire Interviews.* New York: Teacher's College Press.

Heath, S. B. (1999). Rethinking youth transitions [Review of the book *Everyday courage: The lives and stories of urban teenagers*]. *Human Development, 42,* 376–382.

Hebdige, D. (1979). *Subculture: The meaning of style.* London: Methuen.

hooks, b. (1994). *Teaching to transgress: Education as the practice of freedom.* New York: Routledge.

Kirby, D., Kirby, D. L., & Liner, T. (2003). *Inside out: Strategies for teaching writing.* Portsmouth, NH: Heinemann.

Kliebard, H. (1986). *The struggle for the American curriculum 1893–1958.* Boston: Routledge & Kegan Paul.

Kress, G., & van Leeuwen, T. (1996). *Reading images: The grammar of visual design.* London: Routledge.

Lankshear, C., & Knobel, M. (n.d.). *The new literacy studies and the study of new literacies.* Working paper.

Lather, P., & Smithies, C. (1997). *Troubling the angels: Women living with HIV/AIDS.* Boulder, CO: Westview Press.

Lave, J. (1997). The culture of acquisition and the practice of understanding. In D. Kirshner & J. Whitson (Eds.), *Situated cognition: Social, semiotic and psychological perspectives* (pp. 17–36). Mahwah, NJ: Lawrence Erlbaum.

Lave, J., & Wenger, E. (1991). *Situated learning: Legitimate peripheral participation.* Cambridge, UK: Cambridge University Press.

Lemke, J. (1997). Cognition, context, and learning: A social semiotic perspective. In D. Kirshner & J. Whitson (Eds.), *Situated cognition: Social, semiotic and psychological perspectives* (pp. 37–55). Mahwah, NJ: Lawrence Erlbaum.

Lytle, S. (2001). Beyond certainty: Taking an inquiry stance on practice. In A. Lieberman & L. Miller (Eds.), *Teachers caught in the action: Professional development that matters* (chap. 4). New York: Teachers College Press.

Macgillivray, A. (2002). *Bricoleur.* Retrieved July 2006 from http://www.bricoleur.org/archives/000033.html

Males, M. (1999). *Framing youth: 10 myths about the next generation.* Monroe, Maine: Common Courage Press.

Marcus, G. E. (1998). *Ethnography through thick & thin.* Princeton, NJ: Princeton University Press.

McLaren, P. (1994). *Life in schools: An introduction to critical pedagogy in the foundations of education.* New York: Longman.

Meier, D. (2002). *In schools we trust: Creating communities of learning in an era of testing and standardization.* New York: Beacon.

Moje, E. (2002). But where are the youth? On the value of integrating youth culture into literacy theory. *Educational Theory, 52*(1), 97–120.

Perkins, D. (1993). Teaching for understanding. *American Educator: The Professional Journal of the American Federation of Teachers, 17*(3), 8, 28–35.

Phillips, S. A. (1999). *Wallbangin': Graffiti and gangs in L.A.* Chicago: University of Chicago Press.

Polamn, J. L. (2000). *Designing project-based science: Connecting learners through guided inquiry.* New York: Teachers College Press.

Reinsmith, W. (1997). Ten fundamental truths about learning. *The National Teaching and Learning Forum, 6*(5), 7–8.

Ricoeur, P. (1974). *The conflict of interpretations: Essays in hermeneutics.* Evanston, IL: Northwestern University Press.

Rodriquez, L.J. (1994). *Always running: La vida loca: Gang days in L.A.* New York: Touchstone.

Rorty, R. (1999). *Achieving our country: Leftist thought in twentieth-century America.* Cambridge, MA: Harvard University Press.

Said, E. (1996). *Representations of the intellectual: The Reith lectures.* New York: Knopf.

Schultz, K. (1999). Identity narratives: Stories from the lives of urban adolescent females. *Urban Review, 31*(1), 79–106.

Schultz, K. (2003). *Listening: A framework for teaching across differences.* New York: Teachers College Press.

Shultz, J., & Cook-Sather, A. (2001). *In our own words: Students' perspectives on school.* New York: Rowman & Littlefield.

Sitton, T. (1980). The child as informant. The teacher as ethnographer. *Language Arts, 57*(5), 540–545.

Skelton, T. (2001). Girls in the club: Researching working class girls' lives. *Ethics, Place and Environment, 4*(2), 167–173.

Skelton, T., & Valentine, G. (1998). *Cool places: Geographies of youth cultures.* New York: Routledge.

Starnes, B., & Paris, C. (2000). Choosing to learn. *Phi Delta Kappan, 81*(5), 392–397.

Street, B. (2000). Literacy "events" and literacy "practices": Theory and practice in the "new literacy studies." In K. Jones & M. Martin-Jones (Eds.), *Multilingual literacies: Comparative perspectives on research and practice* (chap. 1). Amsterdam: John Benjamins.

Taormino, T., & Green, K. (1997). *A girl's guide to taking over the world: Writings from the girl zine revolution.* New York: St. Martin's Griffin.

Wenger, E. (1998). *Communities of practice: Learning, meaning, and identity.* Cambridge, UK: Cambridge University Press.

Wiggins, G. (1989). The futility of trying to teach everything of importance. *Educational Leadership, 47*(3), 44–48,57–59.

Wiggins, G. (1991). Standards, not standardization: Evoking quality student work. *Educational Leadership, 48*(5), 18–25.

Wiggins, G., & McTighe, J. (2005). *Understanding by design* (2nd ed.). Alexandria, VA: Association for Supervision and Curriculum Development.

Willis, P. (1998). Notes on common culture: Towards a grounded aesthetics. *European Journal of Cultural Studies, 1*(2), 163–176.

Wolf, D. P. (1987). The art of questioning. *Academic Connections*, 1–7.

Woolf, V. (1929). *A room of one's own*. New York: Harcourt Brace.

INDEX

A

Activity, vs. content in learning environments, 35
African American music, history of, ix
Almighty Latin King Nation, 73
Always Running: Gang Days in L.A., 93
Amateurs
  building common culture of, 142–143
  educational value of, 139–140
  teachers as, 137–143
Antisocial, The, 11, 29, 36
Appropriation, 135
  moving from interpretation to, 135–137
  of school space and time for personal work, 160
  by teachers, 150
Archaeology, analogy to turntablism, 106
Art forms
  graffiti writing as, 79–84
  nonmainstream, 7
  subversive nature of, 23
Assessment, 20
  vs. evaluation, 17–18
Attention-deficit disorder (ADD), Ian's diagnosis of, 60–61

B

Beat poetry, and origins of zines, 29
Black Spades tags, 67
Blood In, Blood Out, 93
Brainstorming, in writing process, 4
Breakdancing, 57, 64
  as art form, 7
Bricolage, 38

C

Casa youth center, 79–80
Case study approach, x
  ethnographic, 6
Central Park zine, 31
Chapbooks, 37. *See also* Beat poetry; Zine writing
Church, 124
  negotiation with Gil, 164
  as performance space, 116–118
Civil Rights Movement
  Gil's appropriation of out-of-class learning about, 141
  reinterpretation through turntables, 127–129
Classrooms
  building infrastructure through questions, 151–152
  designing as youthspaces, 23
  developing graffiti writers' skill sets in, 64
Clothing, as performance act, 19
Coleman, Steve, 103–104, 123
  Gil's authority on, 122
  progressive jazz by, 119
  "Tao of Mad Phat," 119, 122–123
Collaboration
  classroom-based, 149–151
  creating in classroom, 9
  imagined forms of, 16
  inherent ethical difficulties in, 12
  in learning, 160
  by teachers with students, 149–151
Cometbus zine, 31
Common culture, Willis's theory of, 3
Communities of practice, 15–16, 20, 34, 51, 61, 136